Projects For Preschoolers

A
Super-Fun
Collection of
Games, Crafts &
Guided Activities
for Young
Children

Suzan W. Allen and Karen H. Talbot
Illustrated by Cindy Decker

International Standard Book Number
0-88290-161-3

Library Congress Catalog Card Number
80-83033

Horizon Publishers Catalog and Order Number
2048

Fourth Printing, May 1987

Printed and Distributed in the
United States of America
by
**Horizon
Publishers &
Distributors**
———————

**P.O. Box 490
50 South 500 West
Bountiful, Utah 84010**

Projects For Preschoolers

About The Book

Projects for Preschoolers is a child's activity book filled with fun and educational projects for pre-school aged children. Although these projects are designed primarily for children four years of age, many of them could be successfully done by a younger or older child.

Each activity is an interesting project that teaches a concept on a preschool level. Some can be done by a child with minimal adult supervision, others require a limited amount of adult preparation. All of them are quick, easy, and entertaining. These projects are actually the visual aids for lessons outlined in a companion volume, *Preparing Preschoolers.* The two books certainly compliment one another, but they could be used separately as well as together. Even if a formal lesson is not taught, a child will both enjoy and benefit from doing the projects in this workbook.

Types of Projects

The projects are both guided and educational, not just busy work. A child will not only have fun, but be learning at the same time or be developing a particular skill. These are worksheets on reading readiness, visual discrimination, numbers, colors, shapes, music, and finishing an unfinished picture—just to name a few. A child will make puppets, hats, paper dolls, charts, games, flashcards, animals, and holiday creations designed especially for the preschoolers' age and capabilities.

Ways to Use This Book

Projects for Preschoolers is designed to be used as a teaching aid by those preparing for or in the process of teaching preschool children—parents, grandparents, teachers, aides, babysitters, church leaders, and others. *Projects for Preschoolers* is ideal for a mother of preschoolers to use in her home. Many mothers in the same neighborhood have found it advantageous to form their own nonprofit preschool or babysitting "pools." Each child could have his own workbook and use it throughout the year as these situations arise. Many school districts are offering preschool cooperative programs where the mother helps with the teaching. This book contains a vast resource of information and ideas that could be drawn upon for this purpose. These projects are ideal to be used in preschools, day-care centers, nursery schools, and church nursery programs. Of course, any child would love a fun project to do on a rainy day or to share with a friend any time.

Activity Numbers Explained

The activity numbers you see on the pages of *Projects for Preschoolers* are a guide back to the lessons in *Preparing Preschoolers.* The code consists of three numbers separated by dashes. The first number refers to the unit number in *Preparing Preschoolers,* the second number refers to the lesson number within the unit, and the third number refers to the activity number within the lesson. (Example: 10-2-4) A table of contents is provided in this book to aid you in finding the art projects you need.

About "Preparing Preschoolers"

This book's companion volume, *Preparing Preschoolers,* is a ready-to-use preschool course. It begins with an introductory chapter that gives valuable, detailed information on how to organize and operate a successful preschool for profit. Information is given on licensing, personnel, physical preparations, insurance, bookkeeping, registration, advertising, rules and regulations, and much more. It can save the inexperienced preschool operator time, money, and help make operating a preschool a successful, rewarding experience.

Next, it contains 14 units of study that are of particular interest to the preschooler. Some of the subjects these units cover are families, community helpers, manners, numbers, colors, music, health and nutrition, animals, seasons and weather, and holidays. Each lesson within the unit has specific objectives and a lesson plan that is easy to follow. Each lesson is carefully written so a child can understand the concepts. The lessons are filled with interesting facts, creative learning activities, suggested arts and crafts, and exciting children's recipes. A separate unit is devoted to a child's physical education needs, with recommended exercises and games. The lessons are self-explanatory. Any adult could teach one of the lessons to a child with only a relatively small amount of preparation time.

Both parents and professionals will be thrilled with the reservoir of information and quality of art work these two books offer, not to mention the countless hours of preparation time that they can save by using these two valuable books.

Contents

A Child's Plea To His Parents

Give me more than food to nourish me. Give me the warmth and the security of your love.

Let me enjoy all five senses. Give me plenty of things to look at, to feel, to smell, to listen to, to taste. And even some things to break.

Teach me to take my turn. Watch me play so you can see how I am trying to work out my problems and what I am up against.

When you tell me to do something, please tell me why I should do it. Let me feel that I am a contributing member of the family. And be sure to include me in making the family plans when you can.

Please don't keep me your baby when I want to feel grown up. Don't transfer your fears to me. I have enough of my own to cope with and I don't need any more.

Help me not to act when I am angry. But don't make me so afraid of showing anger that I lose my capacity to feel strongly about anything.

Let me learn bit by bit to bear pain, to want things but to be strong enough to postpone gratification of certain feelings I am not yet ready to experience.

Let me try out my new powers as my body develops—to creep, to stand, to walk, climb, jump and run when I am ready. Don't limit the natural needs of my body because you have some unresolved hang-ups.

Give me a little corner in the house that is all mine and nobody else's. I need moments of peace and quiet that cannot be invaded by anyone.

Give me my share of consideration and attention. I must know every day, even if for just a few moments, that I am the only one you are thinking about and loving.

Let me ask any question that pops into my head. Don't make me ashamed for having asked it, even if it seems stupid. And give me as honest an answer as you can. If you don't know the answer, please say so. It's good training to hear someone say, "I don't know, but I will try to find out for you."

Be patient with me when I don't do things very well at first. Remember I have so many things to learn and almost everything takes some practice.

Let me bear the consequences for whatever I do. I need to be punished as well as rewarded. And when you punish me, make sure the punishment fits the "crime."

Above all, grant me, without reservation, your debt to me—unconditional love. For if I know it is there, I will be able to give the same to my children—and they will be able to give it to their children.

Your Child

Author Unknown

8

NAME TAG

Color, cut out, write child's name on the apple.

Glue worm and leaf onto apple.

BETTY'S BODY PARTS

Activity 1-2-2

Color, cut out girl. Hook body parts together with brackets.

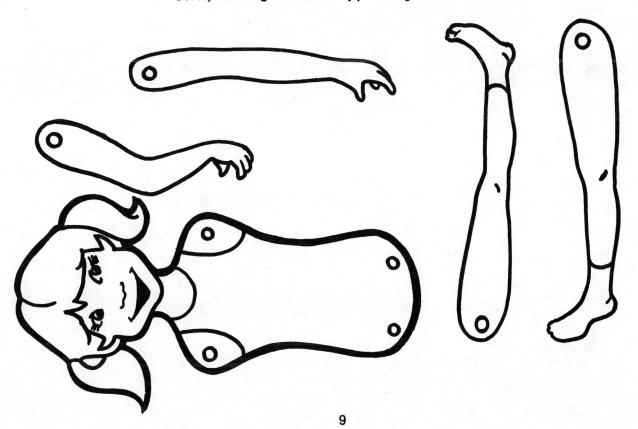

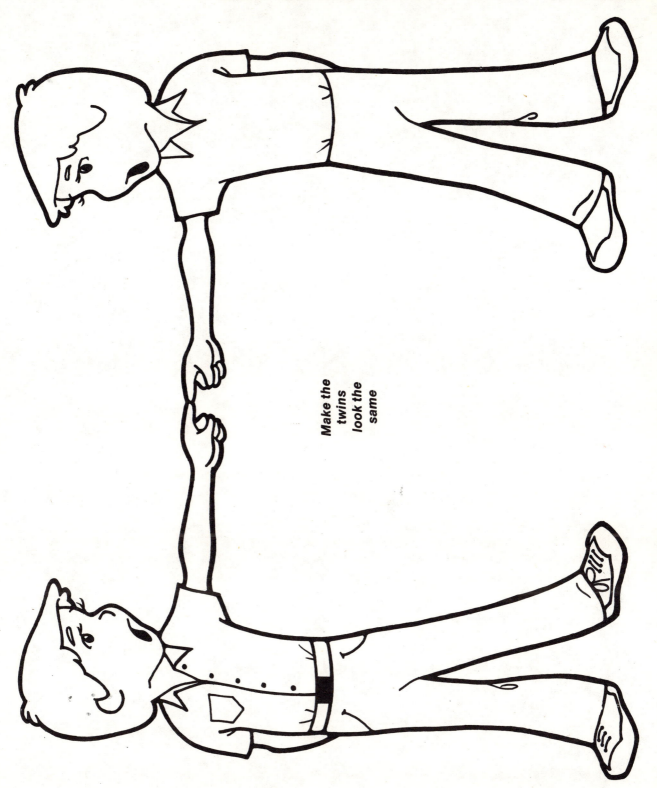

Make the twins look the same

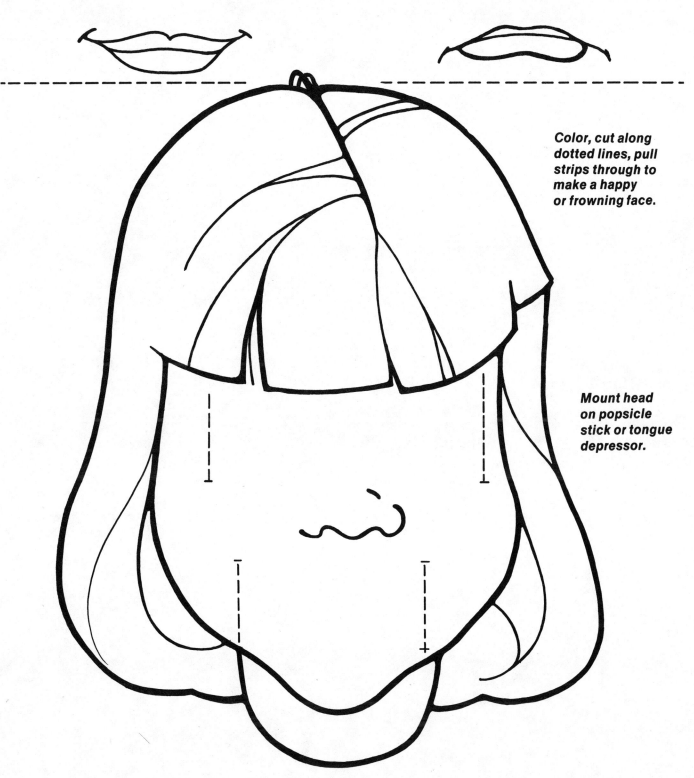

Color, cut along dotted lines, pull strips through to make a happy or frowning face.

Mount head on popsicle stick or tongue depressor.

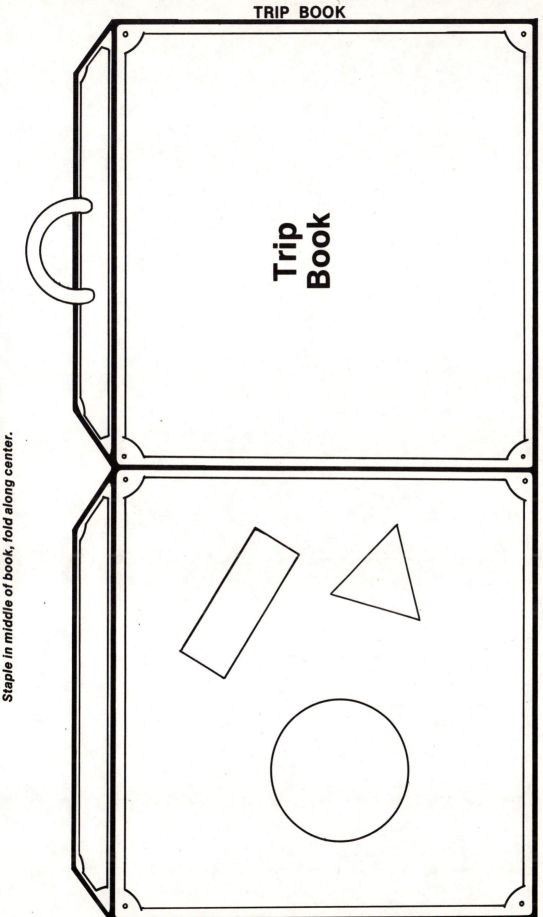

Trip
Book

Color, cut out trip book. Trace outline of trip book on additional sheets.
Staple in middle of book, fold along center.

Cut out pictures from magazines or draw pictures of things he would
like to do with family. Glue pictures inside trip book.

Color and hang up chart. Cut out parent circles And paste on activity when completed with parent.

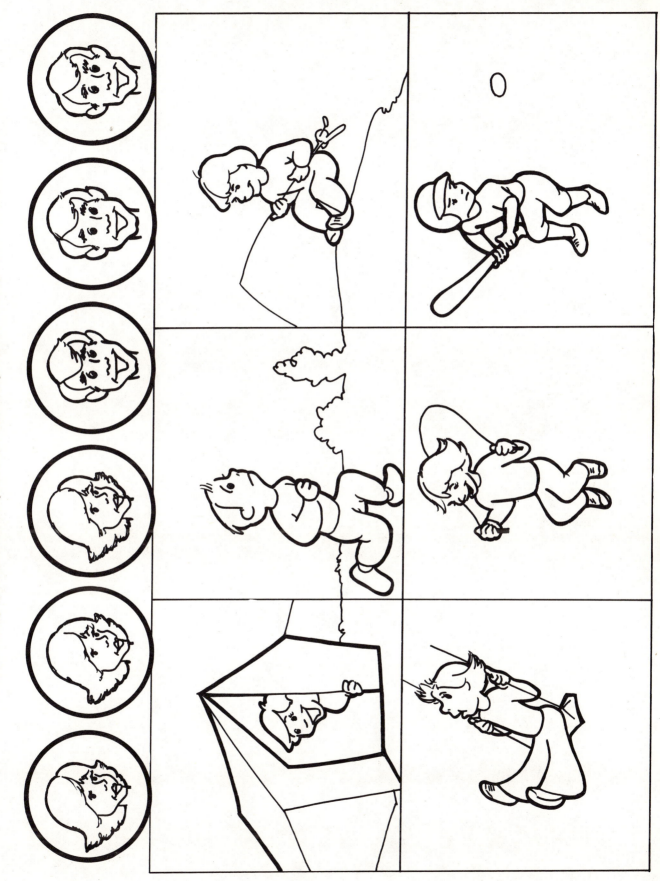

Color, cut out each family member, glue arms together in front to form a circle. Place children inside Mother.

SACK PUPPET (sister)

Color, cut out, paste top half on top of sack. Paste bottom half right under fold.

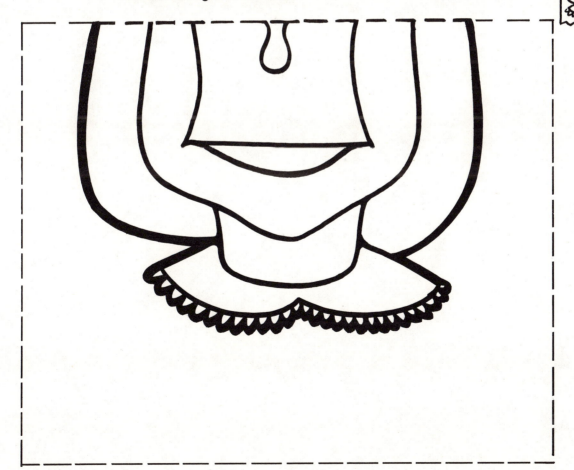

21

*Color, cut out, paste top half on top of sack. Paste
bottom half right under fold.*

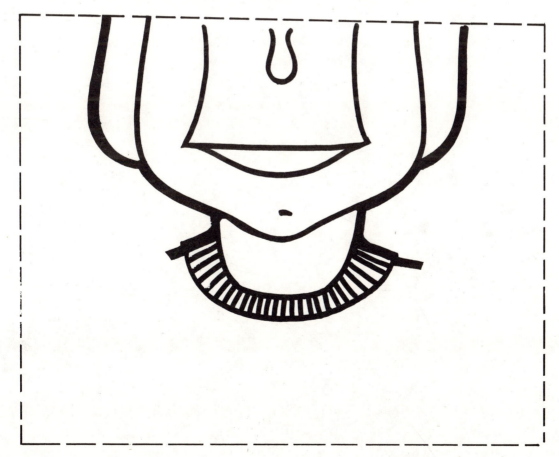

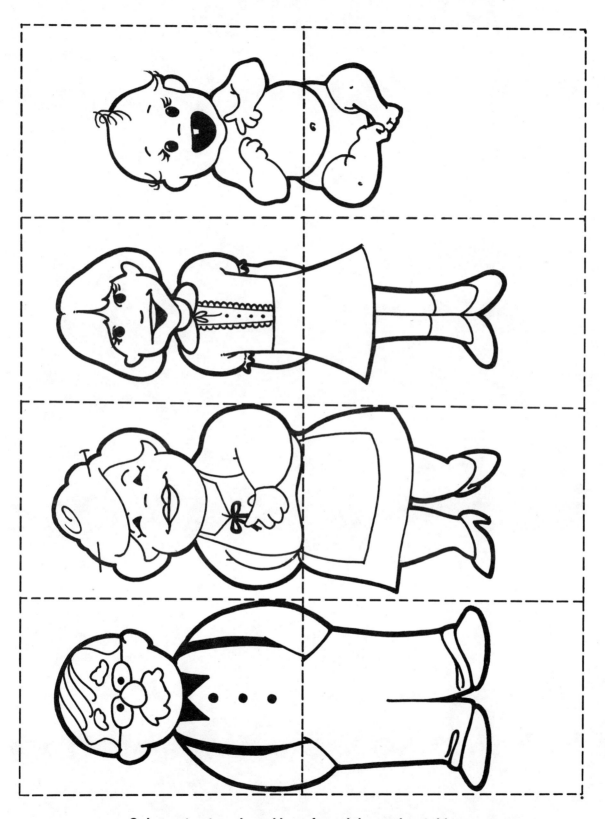

Color, cut out cards and have fun mixing and matching

BABIES IN SEQUENCE

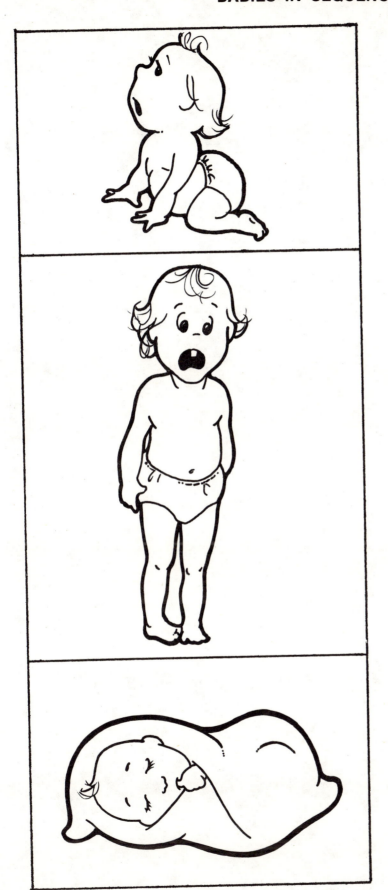

Color, cut out and place babies in proper sequential order.

27

BABY AND ACCESSORIES

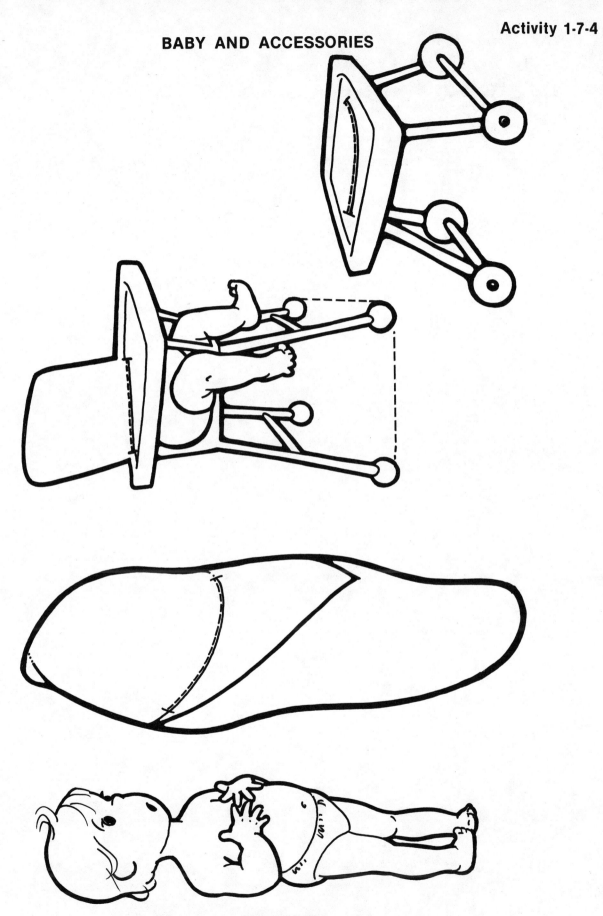

Color, cut out baby and accessories.

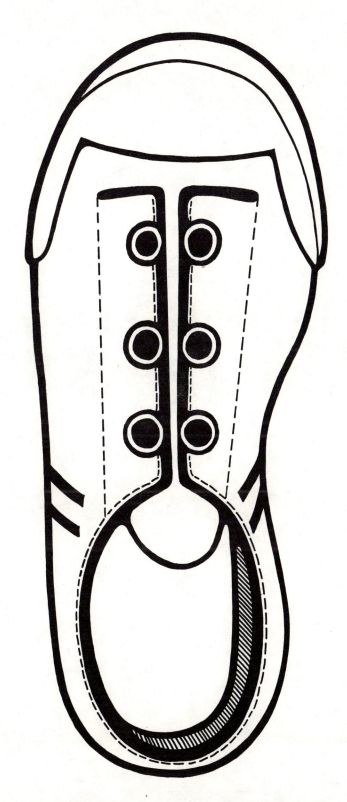

Paste picture on cardboard. Color, cut out shoe. Punch holes for laces, place paper reinforcers over holes. Lace with shoe laces.

SETTING THE TABLE

Cut out parts of a table setting; paste on a plain piece of paper in proper order. Add real napkin to left side.

OCTOPUS JOB CHART

Color, cut out. Attach helping hands when completed to ends of tentacles.

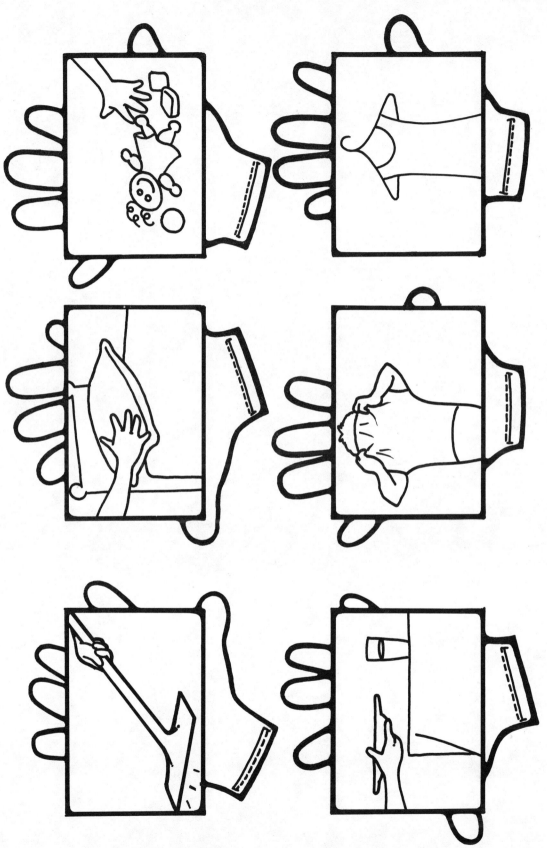

Color, cut out, cut along dotted lines and attach to octopus when activity is completed.

Color, cut out. thread onto piece of yarn or pipe cleaner and tie together.

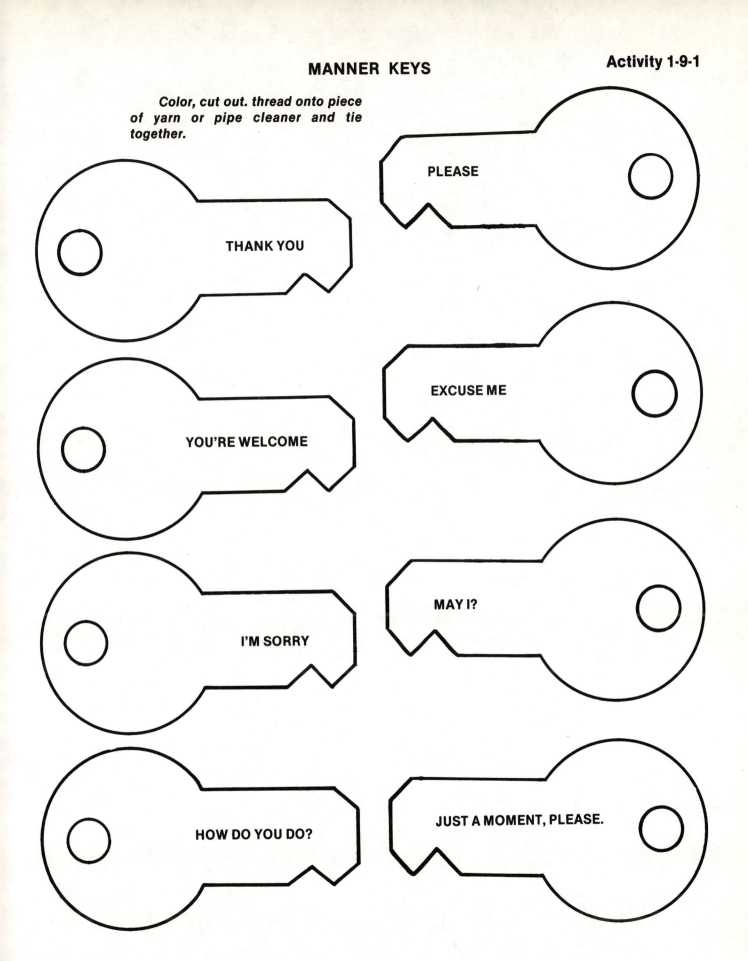

THANK YOU

PLEASE

YOU'RE WELCOME

EXCUSE ME

I'M SORRY

MAY I?

HOW DO YOU DO?

JUST A MOMENT, PLEASE.

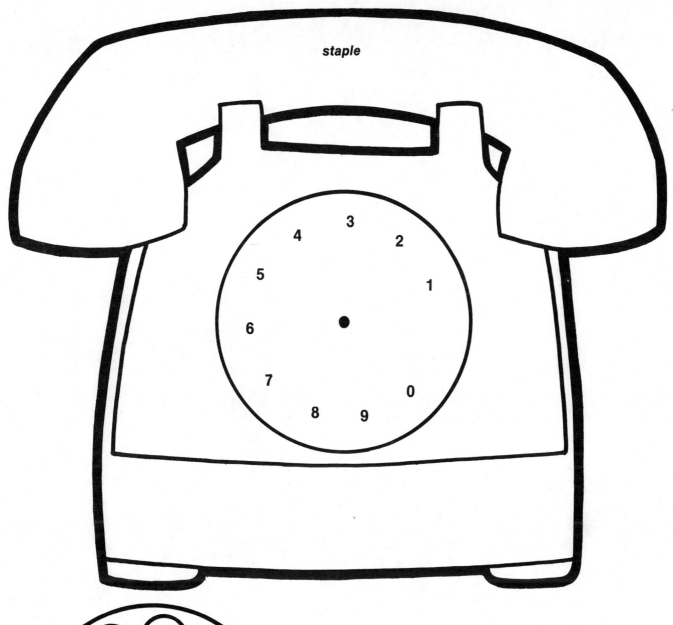

staple

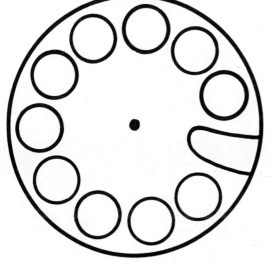

Color, cut out, punch holes in dialer and attach with bracket to phone. Staple additional paper on back of phone for child's number and other numbers.

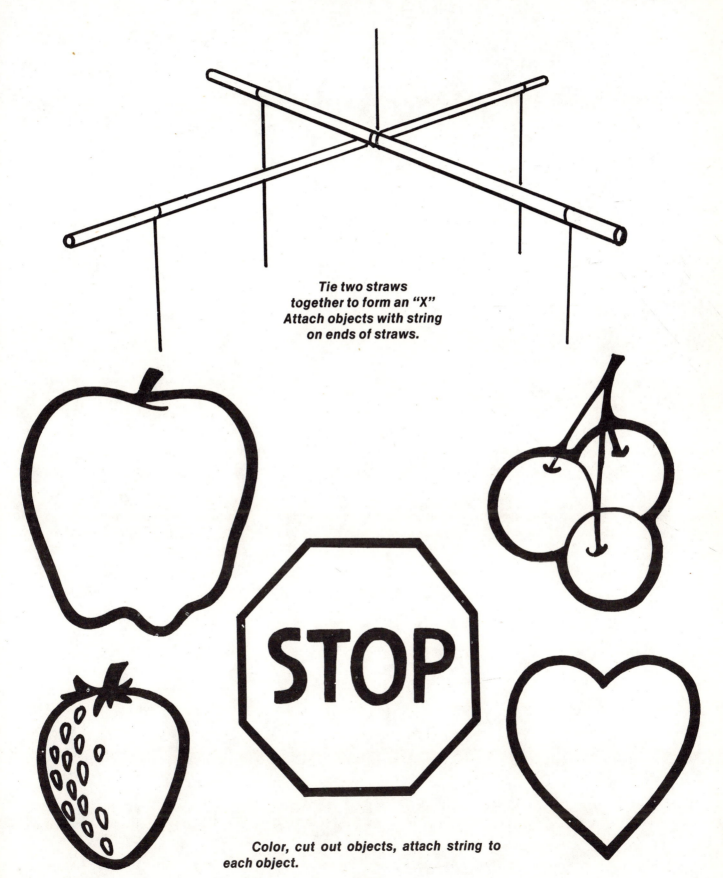

*Tie two straws
together to form an "X"
Attach objects with string
on ends of straws.*

*Color, cut out objects, attach string to
each object.*

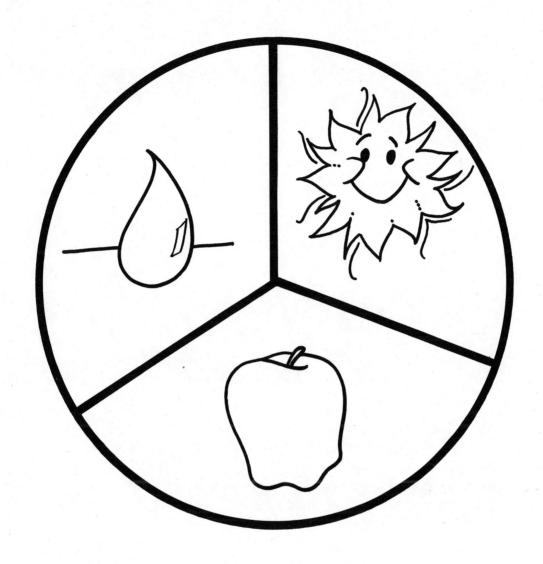

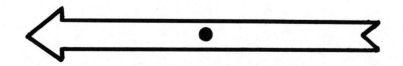

Color, cut out, attach arrow to circle with bracket.

Color, cut out attach
arrow to clown's nose with
bracket.

COLORLAND GAME

START

FINISH

49

Glue stick pretzels for logs onto picture

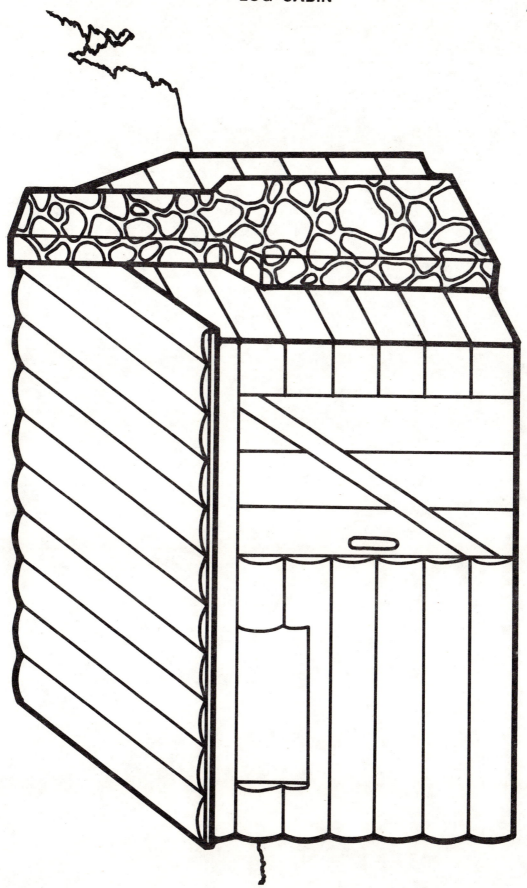

paste

cut

Cut out cars and match with proper sized trailer below.

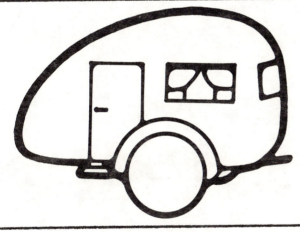

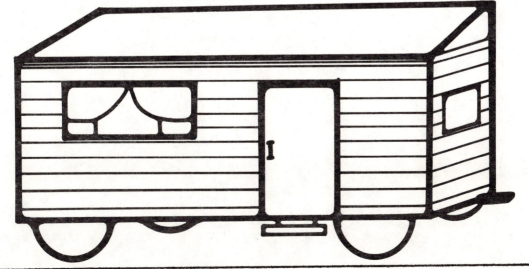

Cut out bricks and paste on dotted lines.

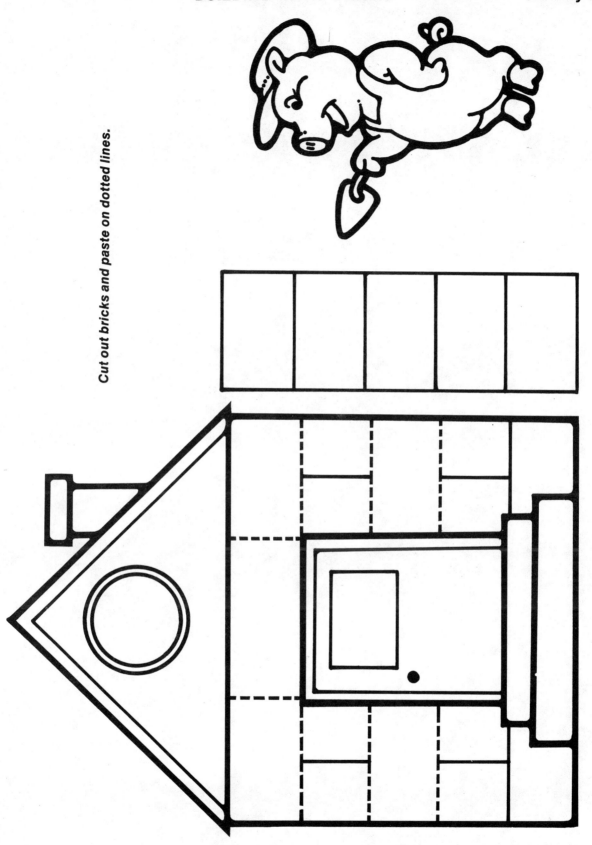

57

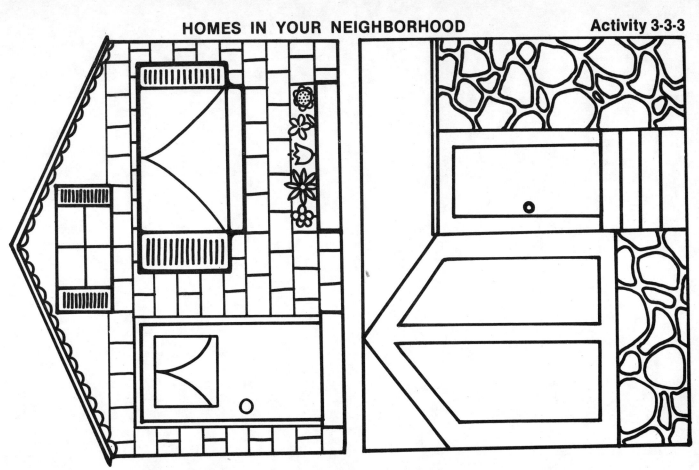

Color and cut out these fronts of houses and paste on jello or pudding boxes and place them around to make a neighborhood.

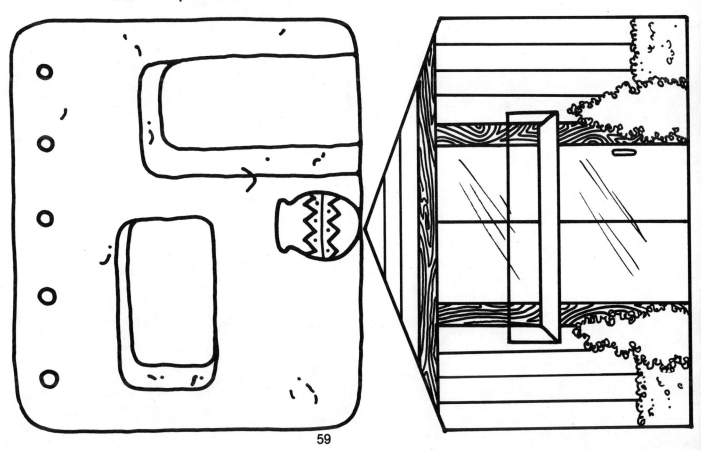

PAPER HOUSE

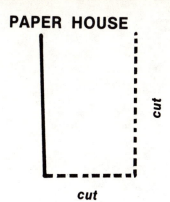

cut

cut

Fold in half first with writing on outside, then fold corner of roof down into house. Fold additional sheets the same way and staple inside for different room. Find furniture on following pages and paste into appropriate rooms.

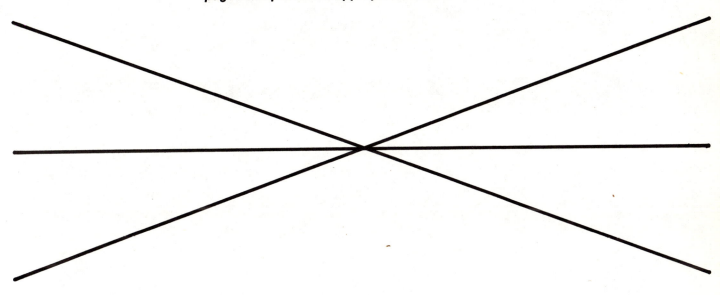

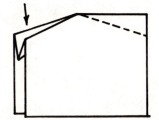

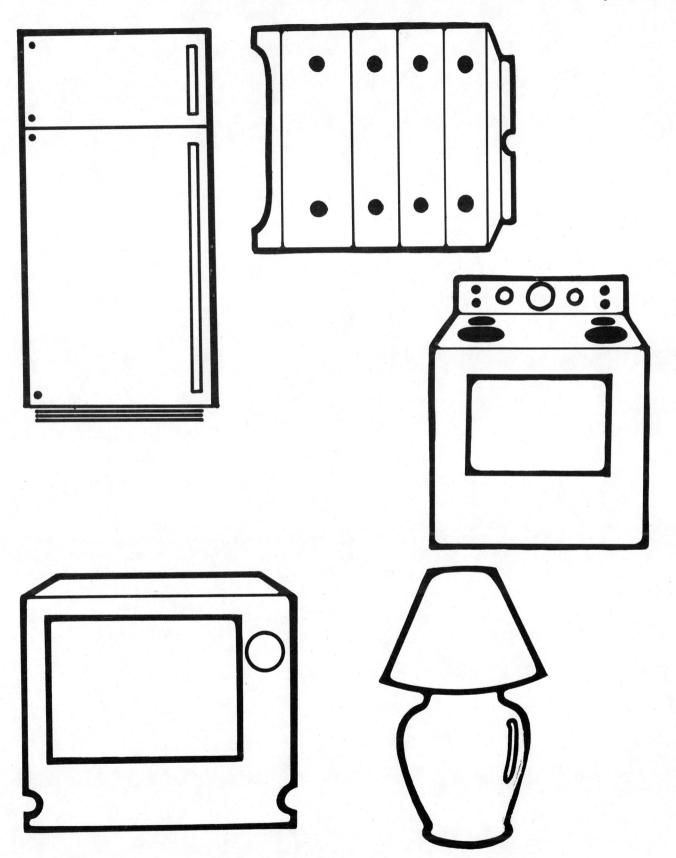

HOUSE TREASURE HUNT

Go on a treasure hunt. When you find these
things in your house, cross them off.

69

OFFICER UGH PUPPET

Color, cut out, paste together as shown in diagram. Paste on popsicle stick.

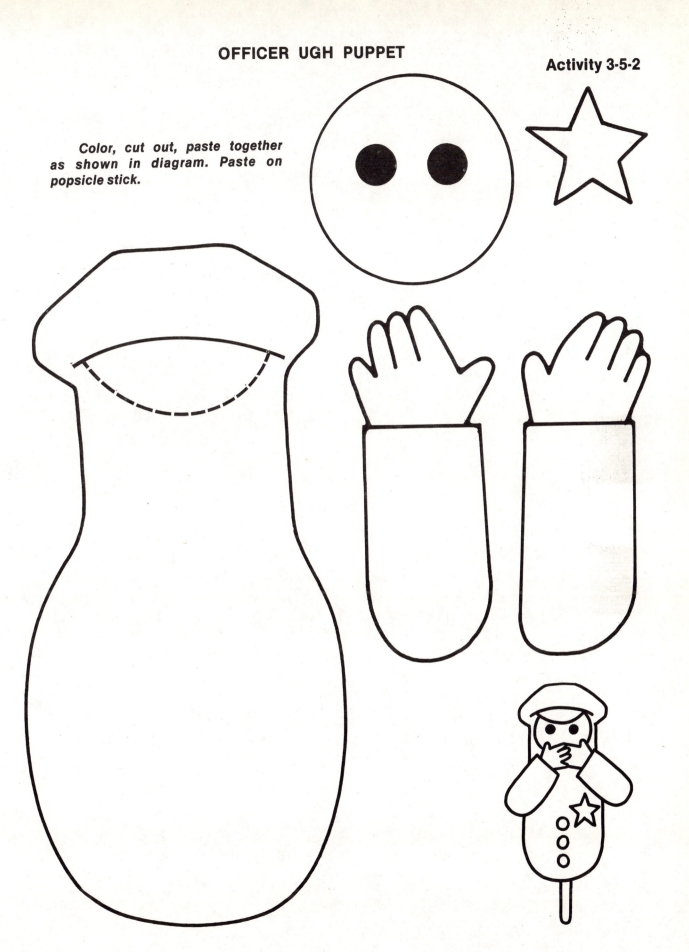

71

CIRCLES AT A BIRTHDAY PARTY

Find the circles in the picture and trace first with finger and then with pencil.

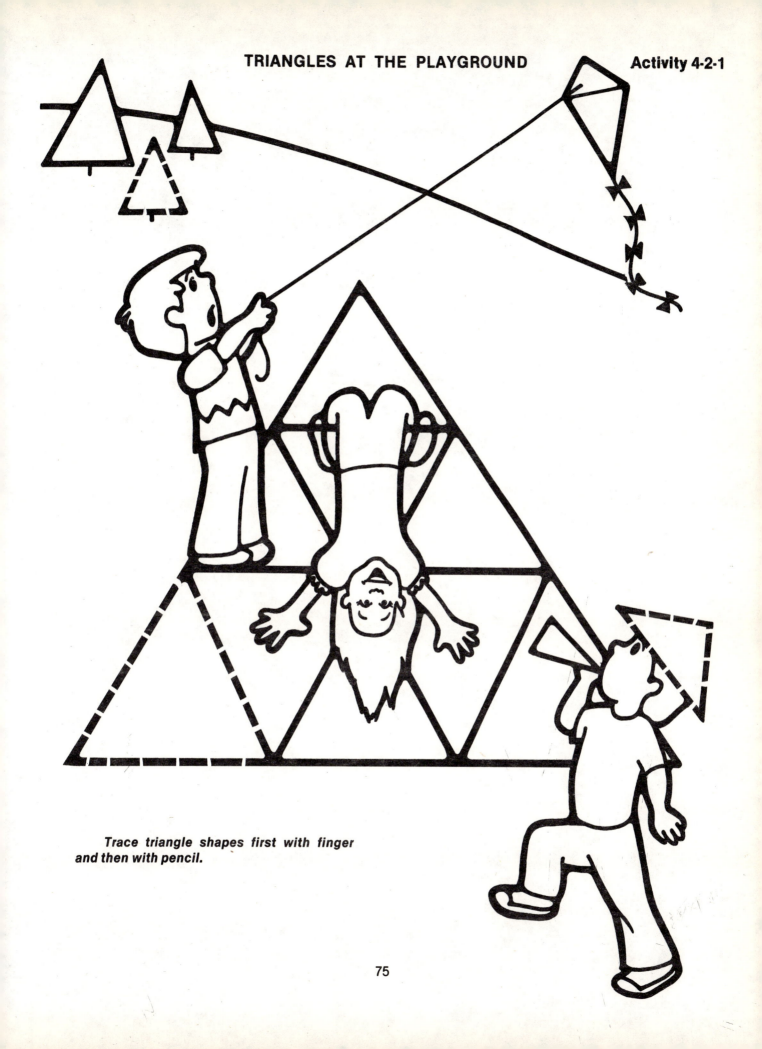

Trace triangle shapes first with finger and then with pencil.

TRIANGLE WORKSHEET

Find the triangle in each row that is facing the same direction as the first triangle in each row.

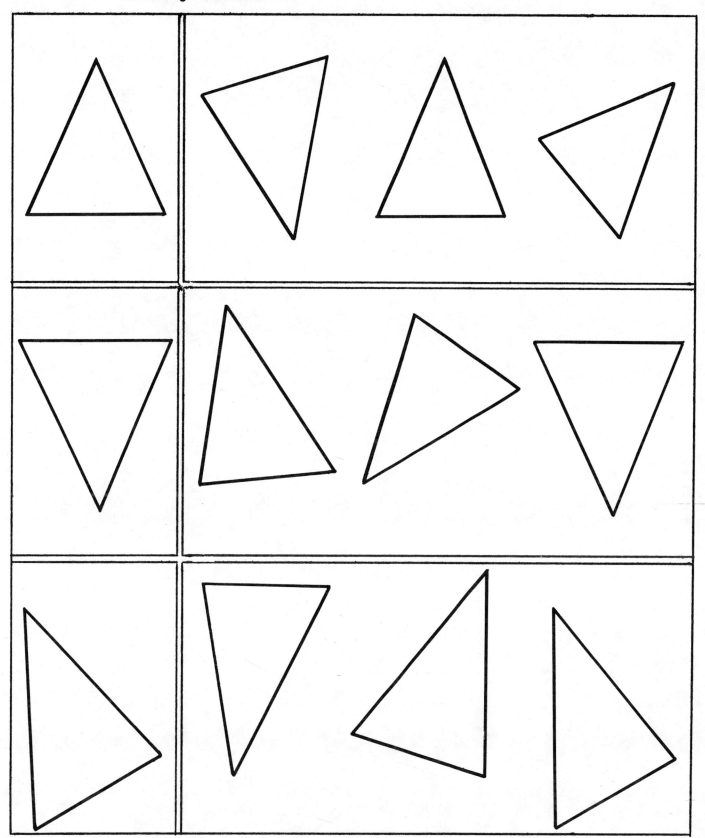

RECTANGLES & SQUARES IN THE PLAYROOM

Find rectangles and squares and trace.

DOGHOUSE MADE OF SQUARES

cut out squares and paste on dog house.

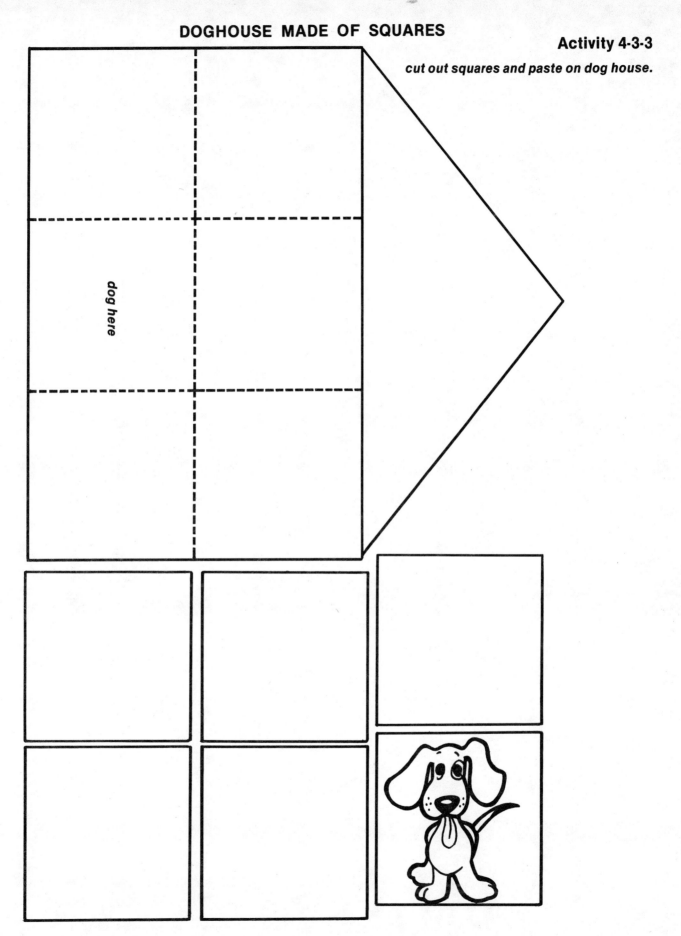

dog here

81

Cut out the shapes below and paste them in the proper shapes above.

Draw a line from the left side to the matching figure on the right.

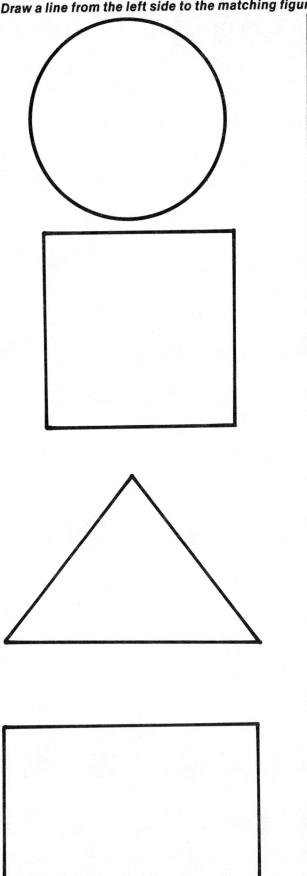

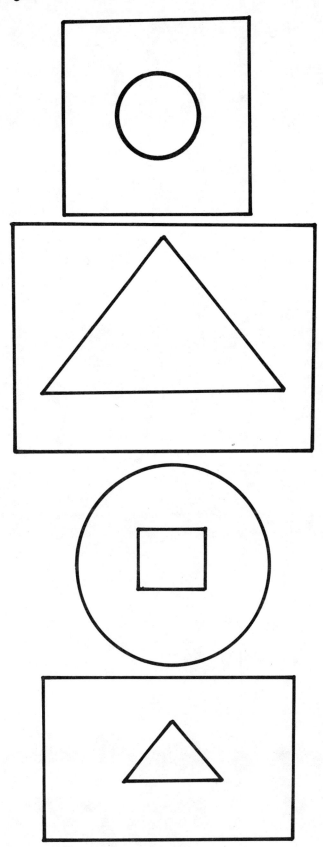

85

SAME & DIFFERENT CONCEPT WORKSHEET

Activity 5-2-9

Cross out the nose in each row that is different from the first nose in each row.

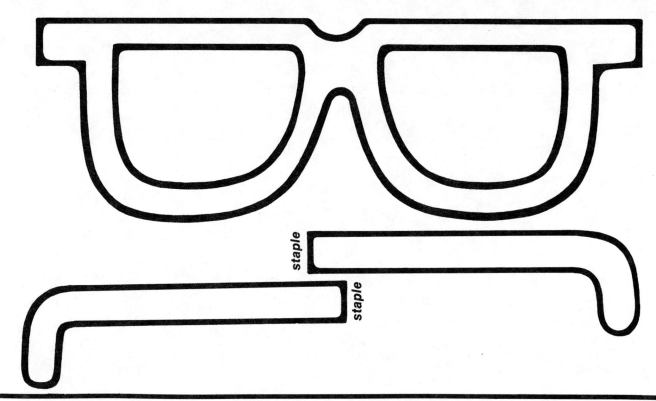

SPECIAL LISTENING EARS

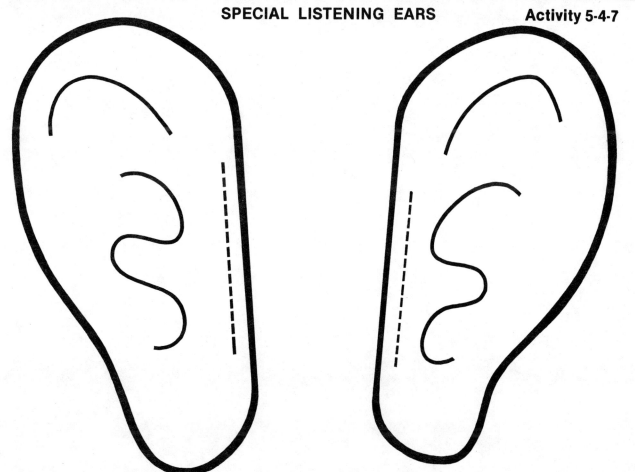

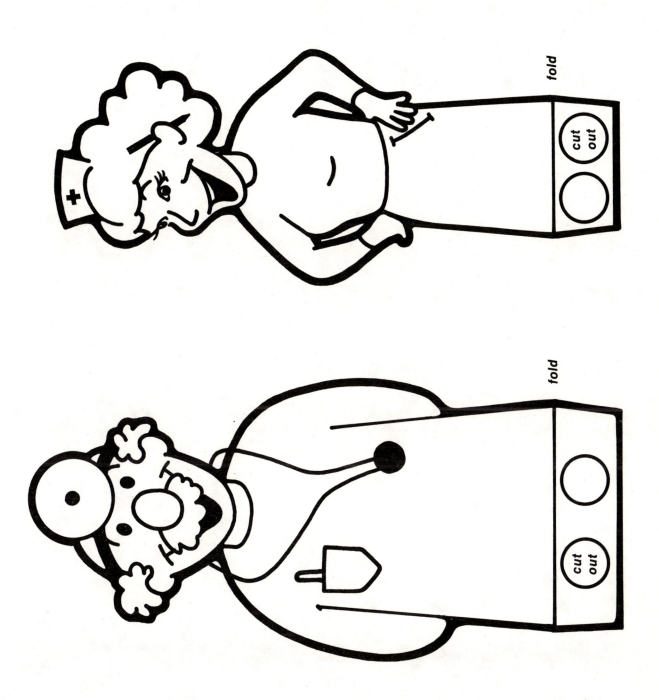

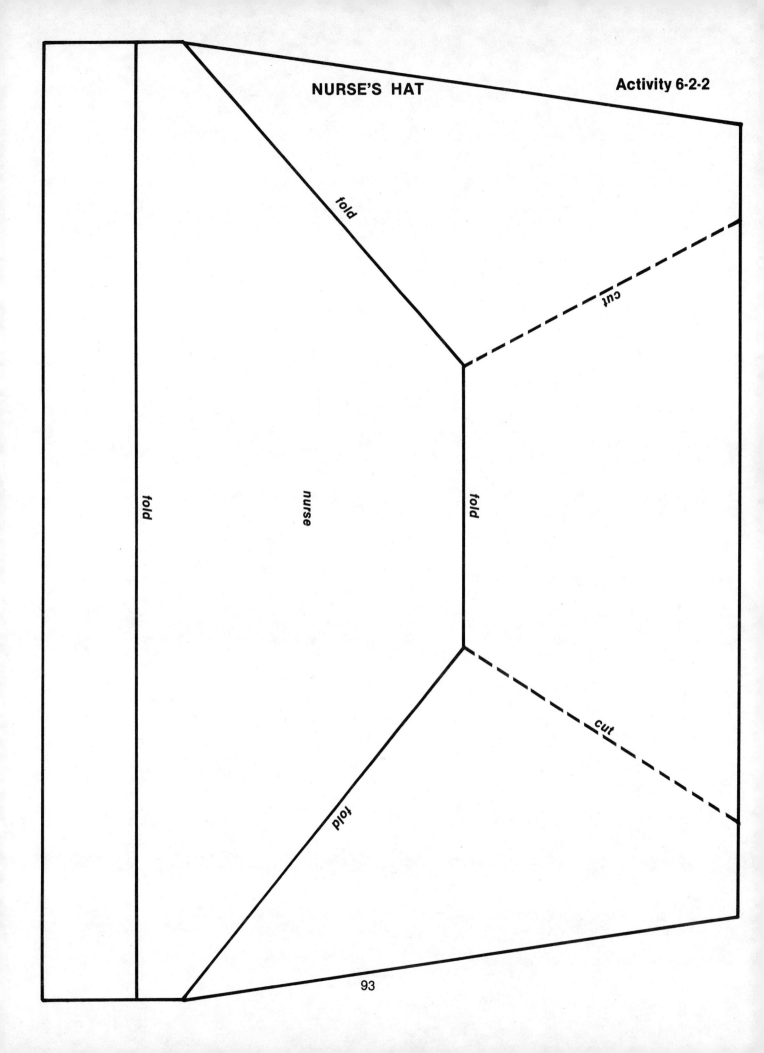

NURSE'S HAT

fold

cut

nurse

fold

fold

cut

fold

93

PHYSICAL FACT SHEET

head size

headsize

chest measurement

chest

waist

waist

shoe size

shoe size

height

height

weight

weight

DOCTOR BAG

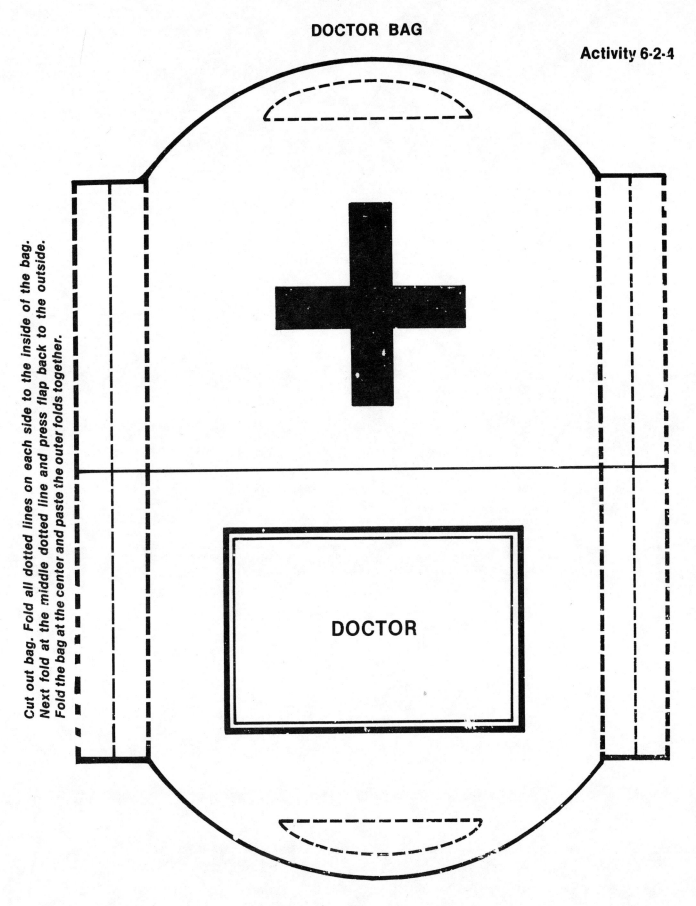

Cut out bag. Fold all dotted lines on each side to the inside of the bag.
Next fold at the middle dotted line and press flap back to the outside.
Fold the bag at the center and paste the outer folds together.

DOCTOR

POLICEMAN PUPPET PATTERN

Activity 6-3-1

face

gold
star

paper
reinforcers
for buttons

Use this pattern to make a policeman puppet out of felt.

STEPS TO CROSSING THE STREET

1. Walk to the corner or crosswalk.

2. Stop before you begin to cross.

3. Look both ways.

4. Walk across the street.

Cut out, paste in proper order for crossing the street.

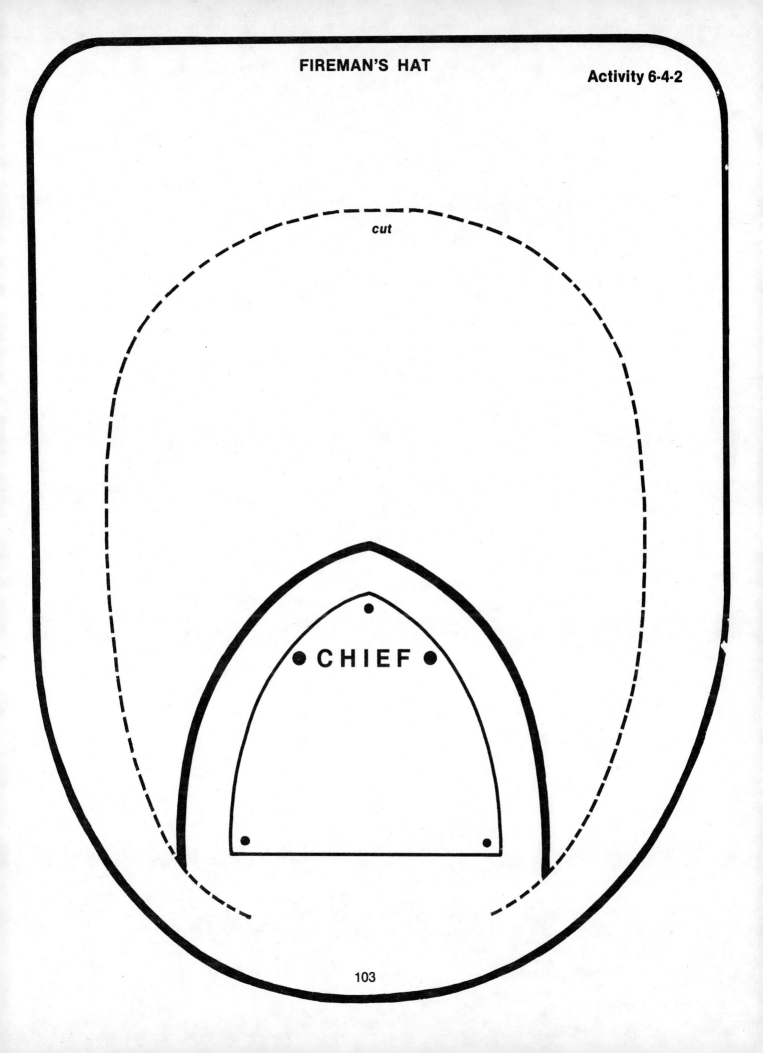

FIREMAN'S HAT

cut

CHIEF

FIRETRUCK PUZZLE

FIRE TRUCK

Cut out parts and paste on truck

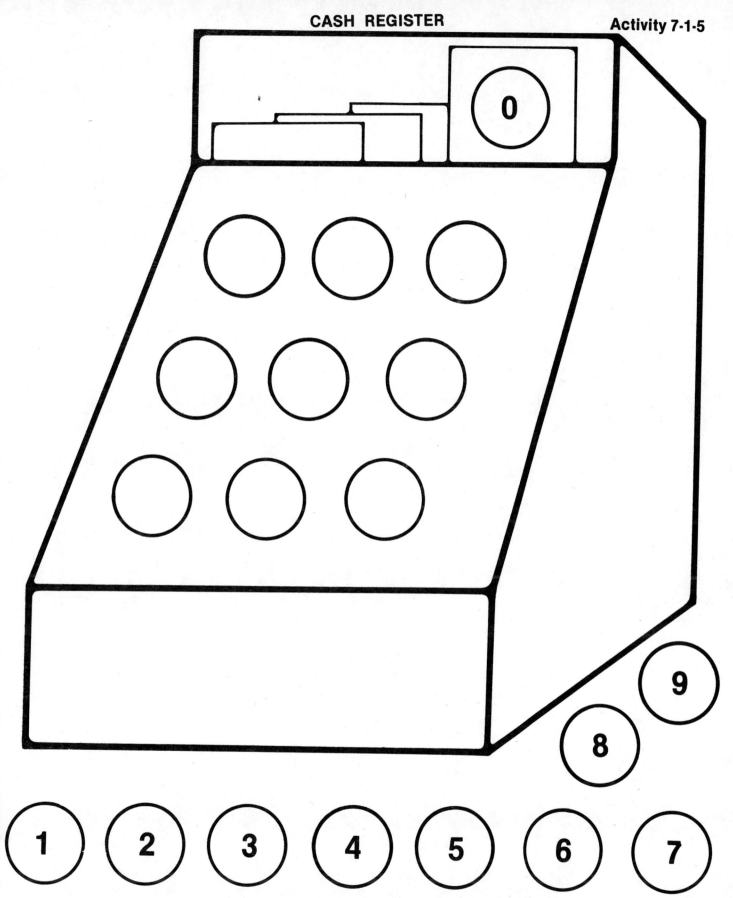

Cut out numbers and paste in order on cash register, left to right.

TRAIN PATTERNS

Activity 7-1-6

Cut out on colored paper so you have 10 cars. Number the cars 1-10 and staple them in order.

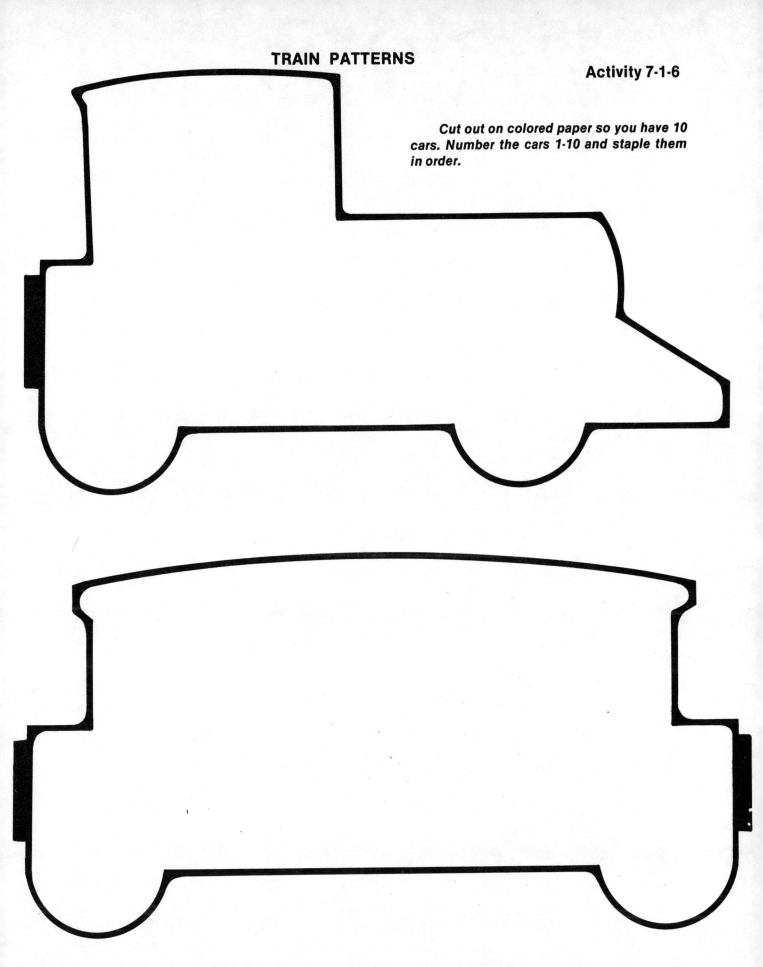

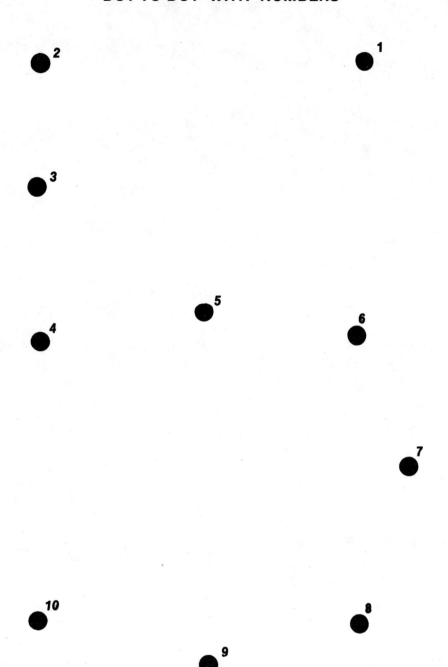

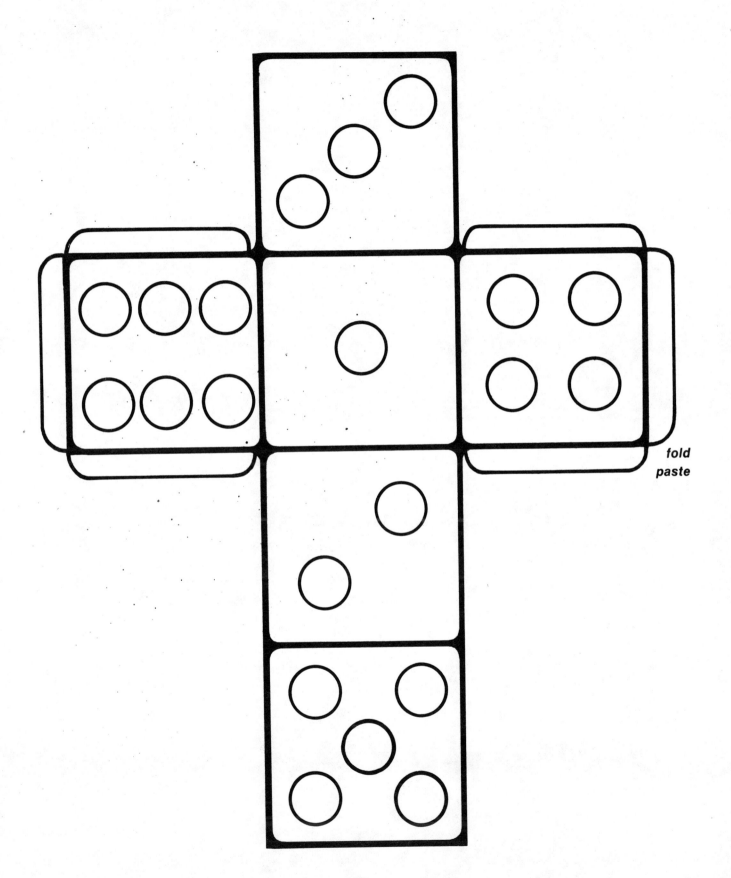

fold
paste

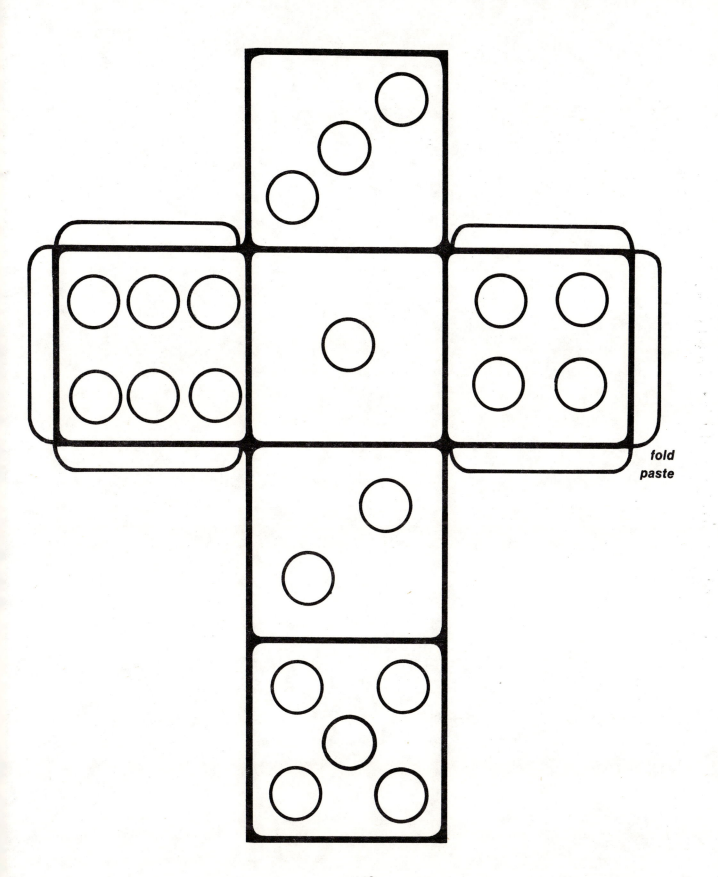

fold
paste

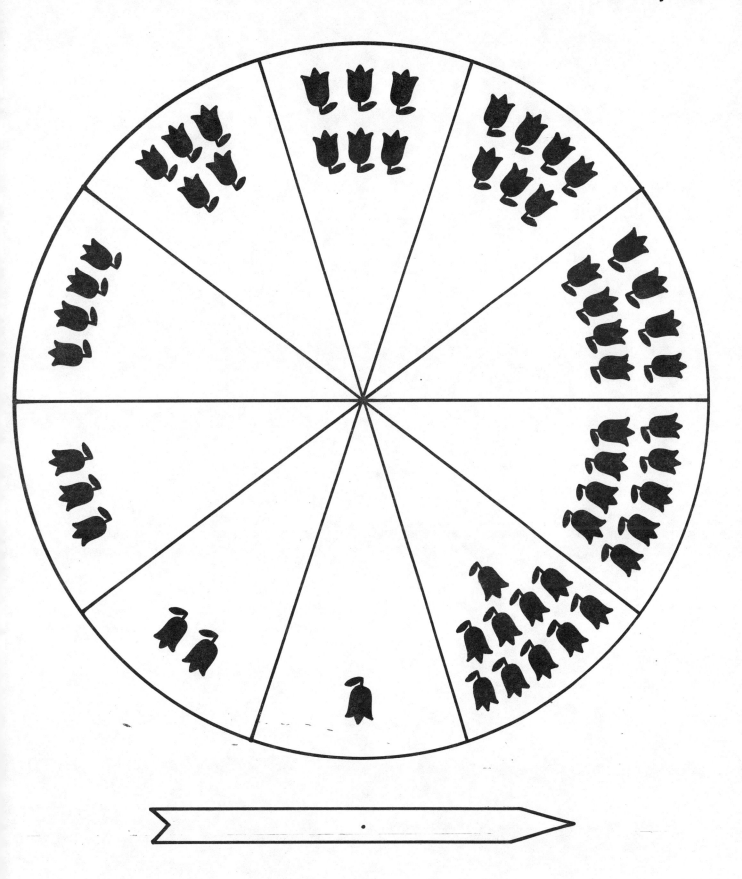

NUMBER WORKSHEET

Draw a line from each number on the left to the proper number of objects it represents on the right.

1	
2	
3	
4	

Cut out the bowls and spoons and paste under each bear according to proper size.

GROWING GIRAFFE

Color and cut out giraffe. Put giraffe's neck in slot and make it grow longer and shorter as moved.

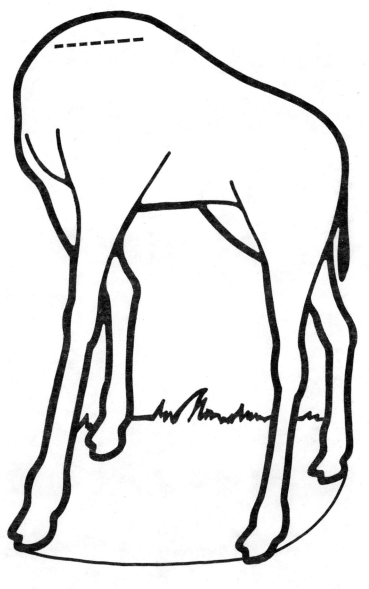

127

FOUR BASIC FOOD GROUPS CAROUSEL

Bracket

129

Paste different grains to fill in little Red Hen; such as popcorn, wheat, rice, peas, beans, etc.

MILK SEQUENCE WORKSHEET

1.

2.

3.

4.

Color, cut out each picture and place in sequential order.

MILK PRODUCTS PULL-THROUGH

Cut out strips of dairy products and let child pull the strips through the milk bottle and name each product.

VEGETABLE CREATURE

Make a vegetable creature by cutting out the vegetables and gluing in shape on a piece of paper.

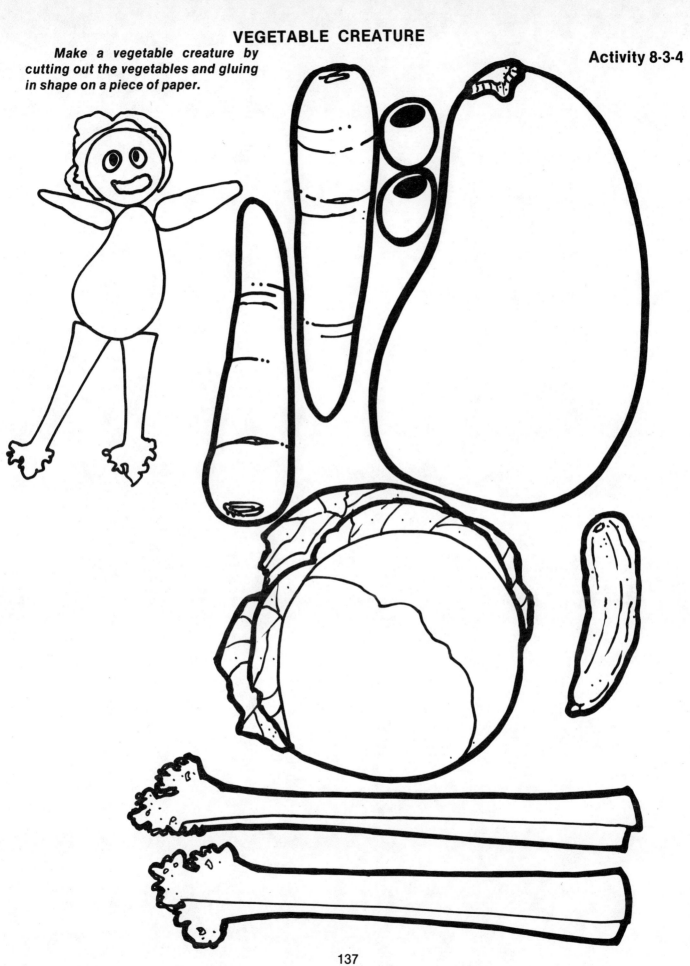

137

VEGETABLE GARDEN WORKSHEET
(Same & Different Concept)

Make an "X" on the object that is not a vegetable on each row.

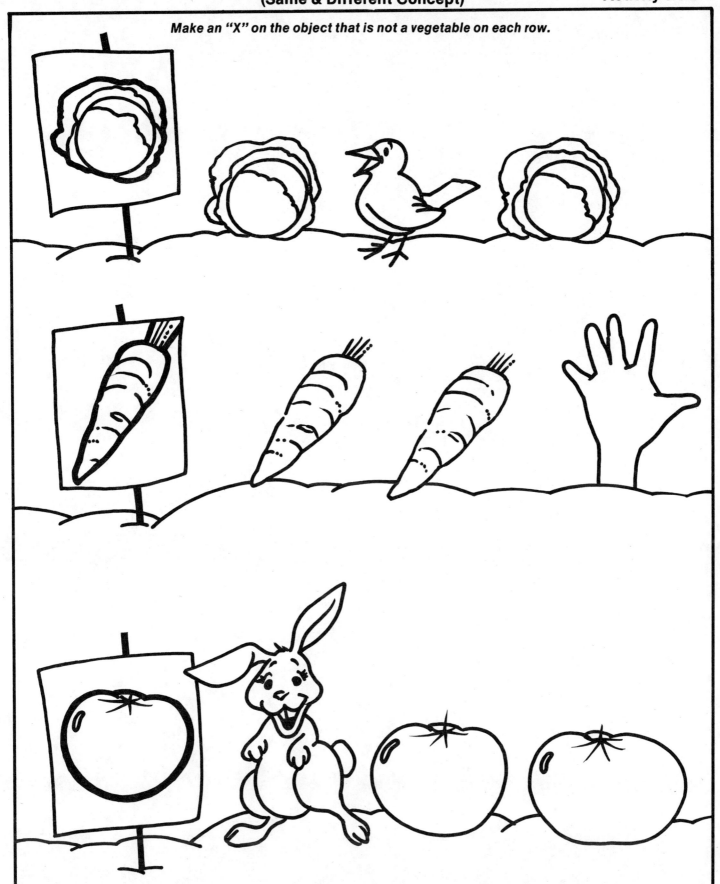

PEAS IN A POD

Color the peas, paste them in the pod, and fold the pod over.

Color the fruit, cut out, and paste on the tree.

Draw a line from the left to the right food the animal gives us on the right.

Color, cut out and paste onto two sheets—
One for night (black) and one for day (blue).

THREE BEARS WORKSHEET
(Size Concept)
Dress each bear by pasting on their pajamas. Paste each bear in his properly sized bed.

Activity 8-6-3A

THREE BEARS' BEDS

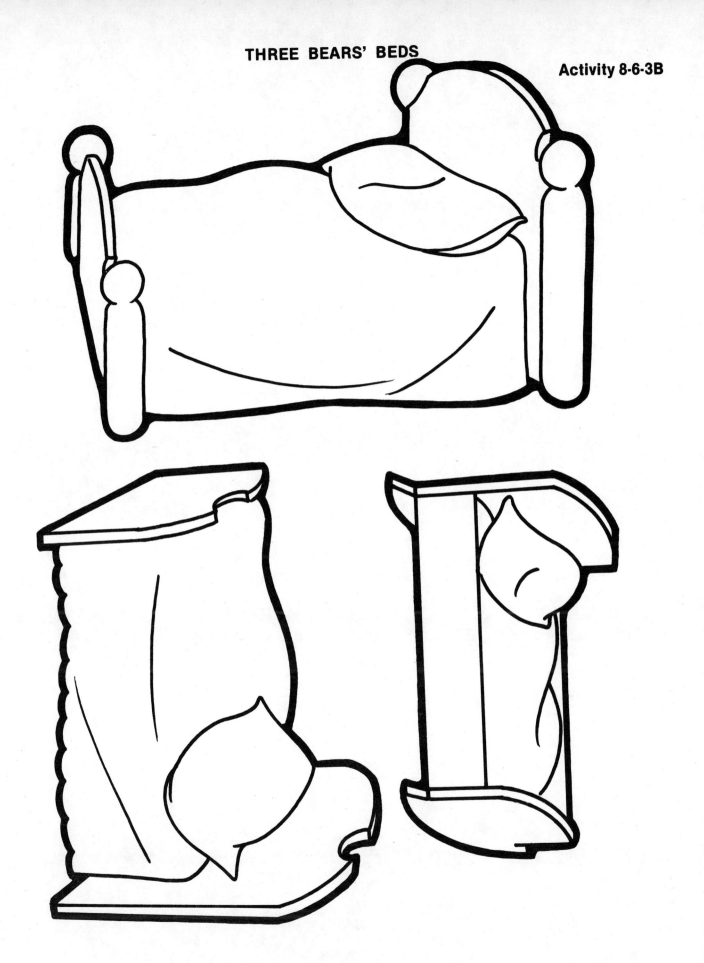

SLEEPING BOY

Color, cut out, and cut slits for eyes. Push eyes into the slits from the back. Moving the eyes up and down will open and close eyes.

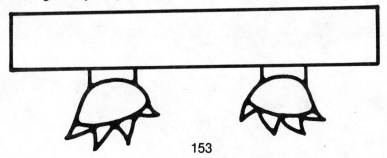

THREE MEN IN A TUB

Activity 8-7-2

Color, cut out, and paste three men in the tub.

GROOMING CHART

Activity 8-7-3

Let the child place a check or star in each square when he has completed each grooming task daily.

CLEANING UP THE KIDS

Clean up the kids by pasting on the clean parts.

159

Place bandaids over the places where the child is injured.

Color the animals and then trace the path of each animal.

CARS

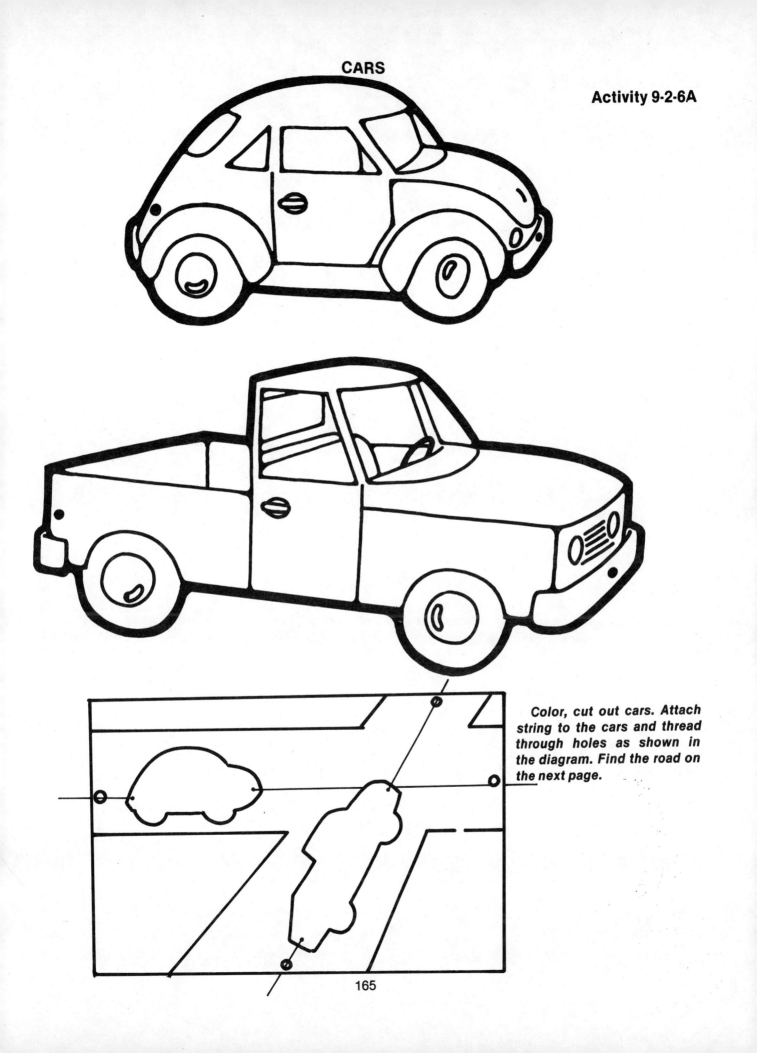

Color, cut out cars. Attach string to the cars and thread through holes as shown in the diagram. Find the road on the next page.

165

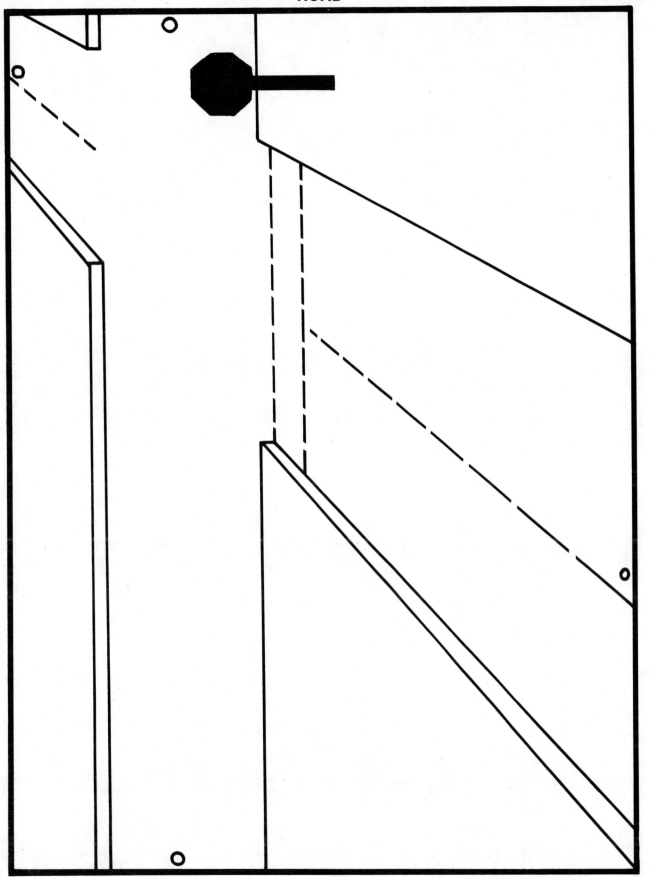

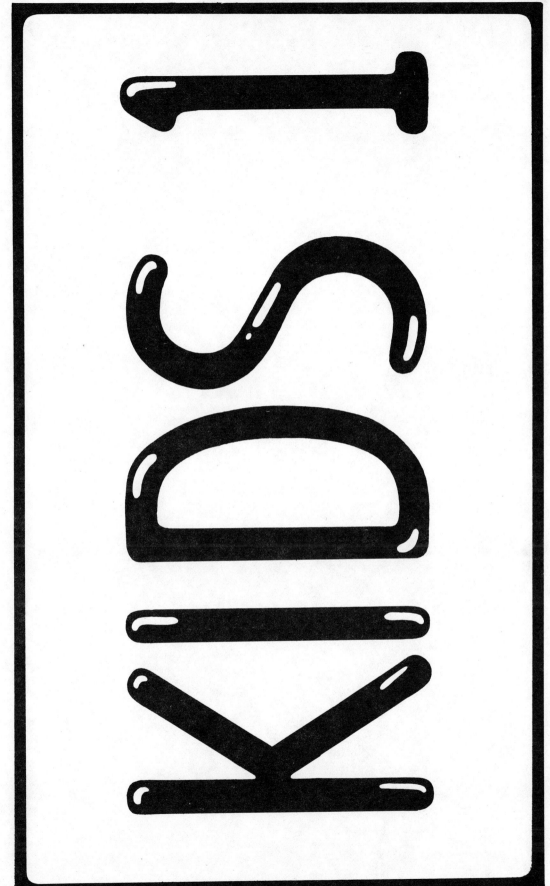

Attach license plate to bicycle.

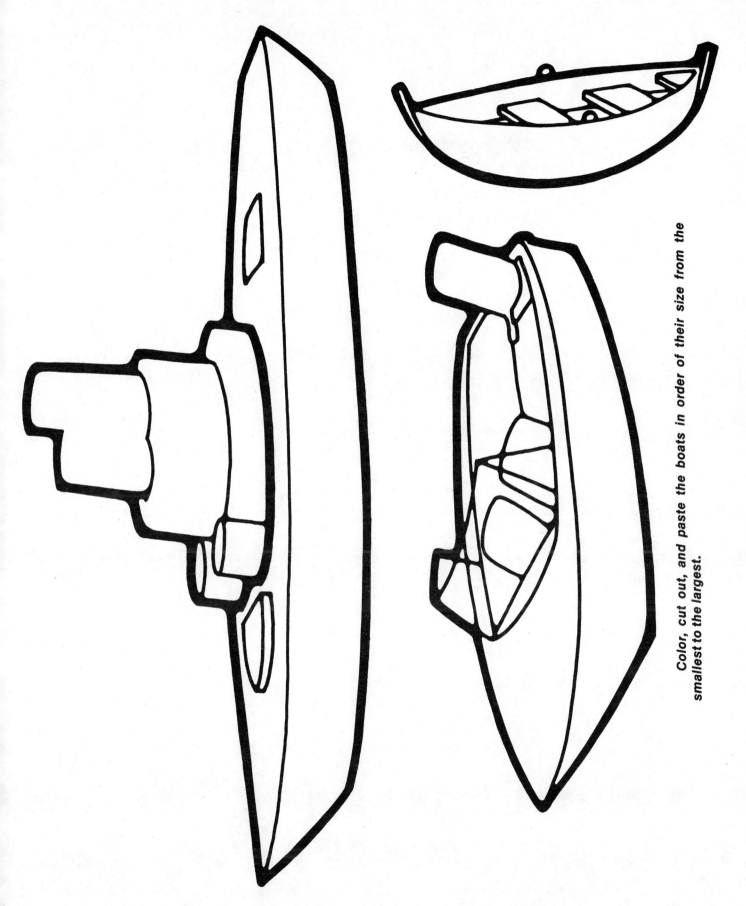

Color, cut out, and paste the boats in order of their size from the smallest to the largest.

ENGINEER HAT, WATCH & BADGE

Activity 9-4-1

Activity 9-4-3

Make a paper chain out of construction paper and attach to the conductor's watch.

Activity 9-4-4

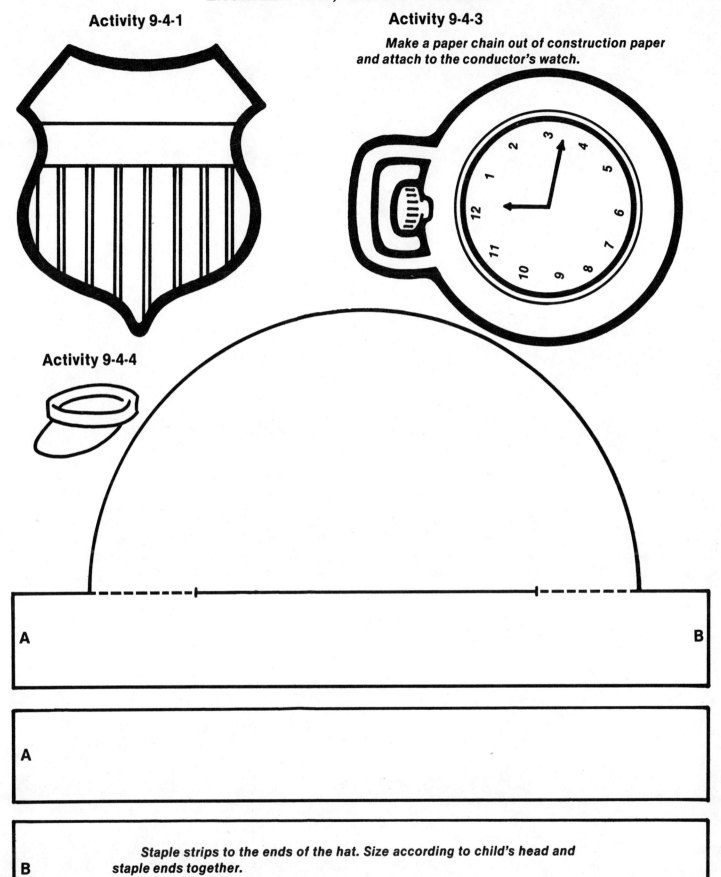

A

B

A

B

Staple strips to the ends of the hat. Size according to child's head and staple ends together.

PAPER GLIDER & HELICOPTER

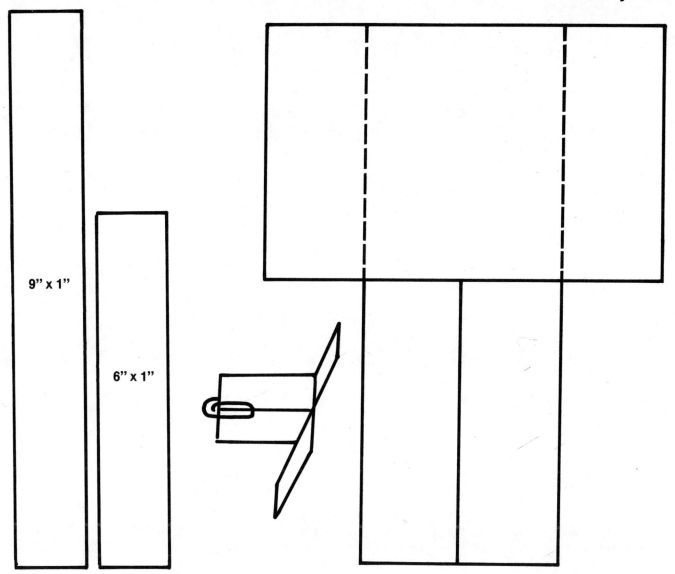

9" x 1"

6" x 1"

Cut out, fold, attach paper clip as shown and drop.

PAPER GLIDER

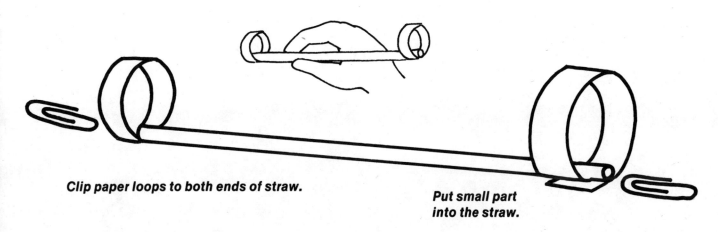

Clip paper loops to both ends of straw.

Put small part into the straw.

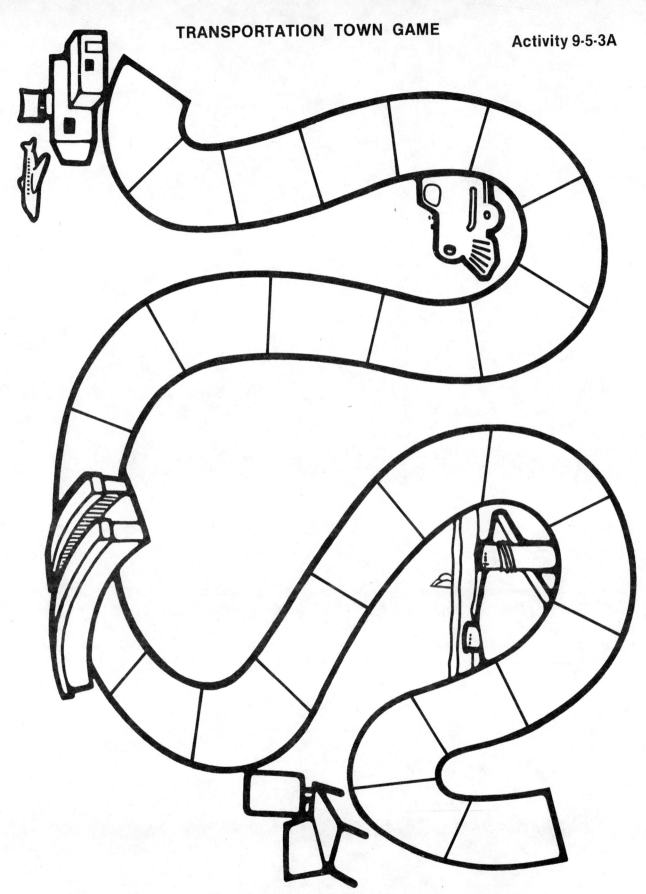

Use dice as spinner and advance airplane in spaces as indicated by number on dice. First one to the airport wins.

177

ELEPHANT STRAW

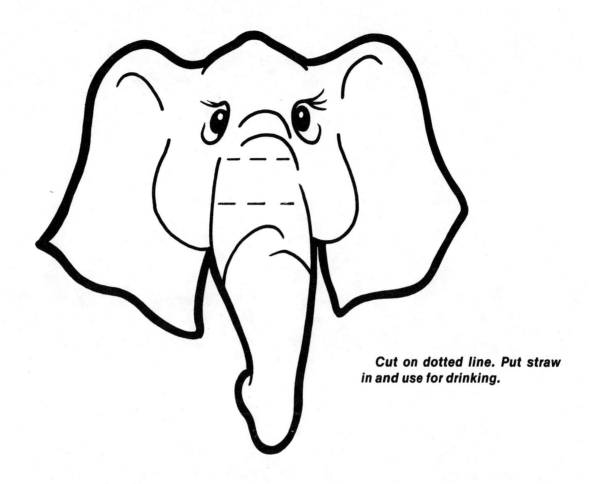

Cut on dotted line. Put straw in and use for drinking.

Movers for Transportation Town Game on previous page.

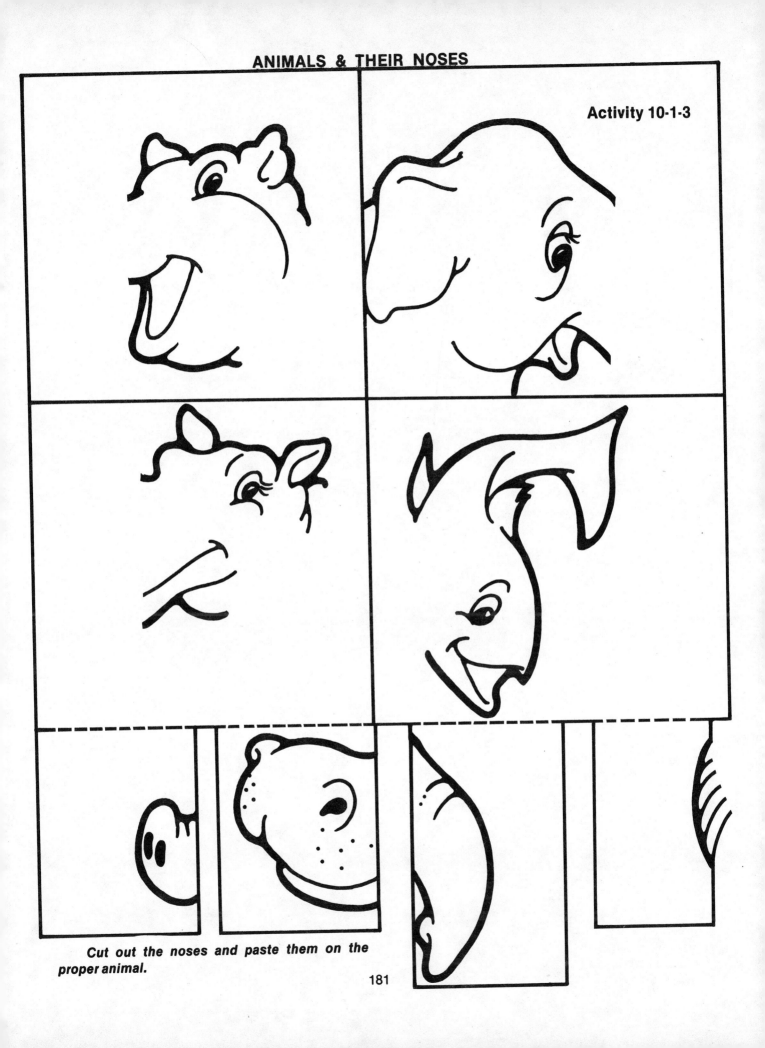

Activity 10-1-3

Cut out the noses and paste them on the proper animal.

181

ANIMAL HAT

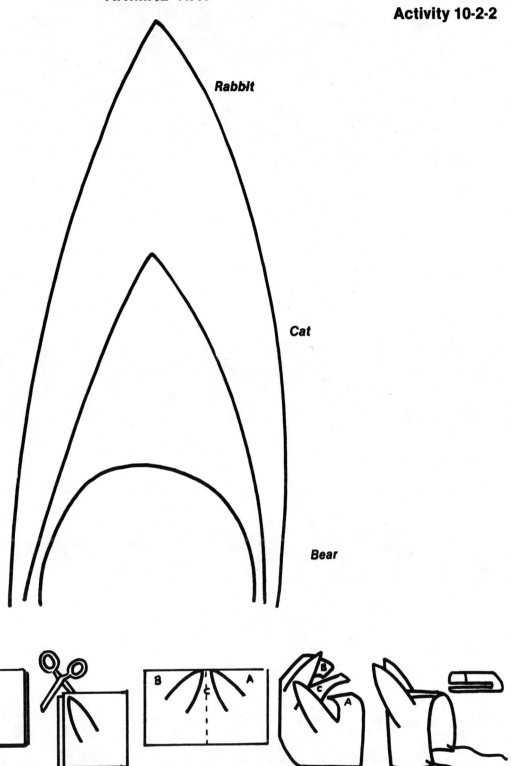

Rabbit

Cat

Bear

Using an 11″ × 17″ sheet of paper (or two 8½″ × 11″ stapled together), fold in half to 8½″ × 11″, place pattern of ears over the folded sheet so that the desired ear is flush with the edge of the folded paper. Cut out desired shape. Open the folded paper and bend C section forward. Holding C section in place, bend section A and B underneath C and overlap A and B until the hat is formed. Staple A, B and C together on front edge. Attach yarn or string at bottom corners for ties.

183

ANIMALS & THEIR FEET

Cut out the two rows of feet. Slide through slots on animals to find the proper pair of feet.

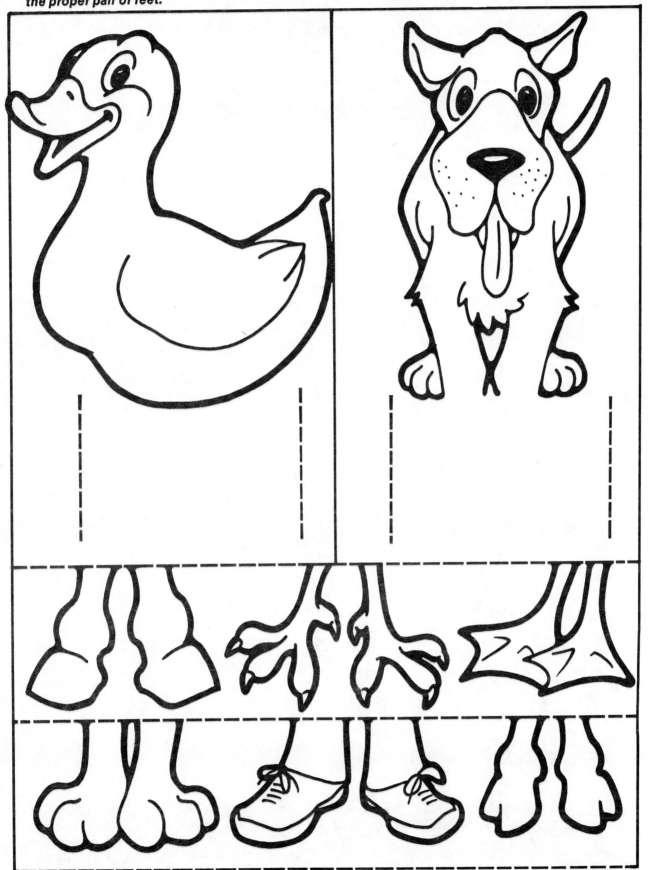

ANIMAL FLASH CARDS

Color the cards, cut on dotted and solid lines. Match up bottoms and tops of the animals.

187

ANIMALS & THEIR TAILS

Paste the tail on the proper animal.

SAINT BERNARD DOG

Activity 10-3-2

Back view

Brackets

String

CAT & WHISKERS

Fold whiskers accordion style and put in slots. Color and cut out cat.

Activity 10-4-1

195

ANIMALS & THEIR BABIES

Draw a line from each mother to her lost baby.

MOTHER RABBIT & BABY BUNNIES

Paste a small envelope on the back of the mother rabbit and place her babies in the envelope.

Cut out and fold pigs along dotted lines to stand up.

KANGAROO & BABY

Cut pouch on dotted line and place baby inside.

Draw a line from each animal to its proper home.

205

UNDERGROUND ANIMAL HOMES

Draw a line starting from the left to show the animal the way out of his underground home.

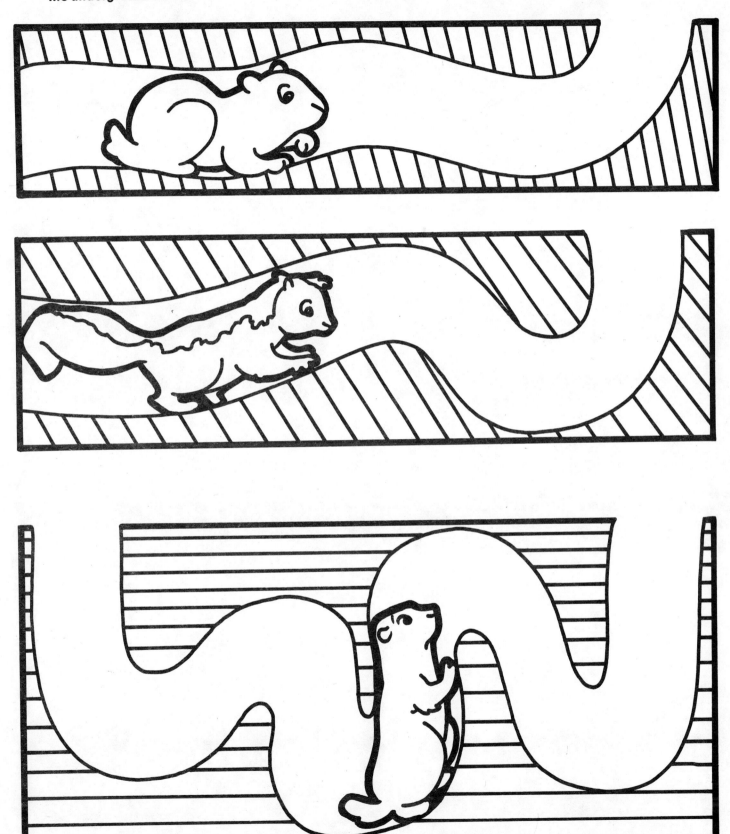

FROG & TURTLE RACE

Color, cut out frog and turtle. Punch hole. Using about 12 feet of string tie one end to a chair or table leg. Thread the other end through the frog or turtle. By pulling tight and letting go and moving up and down, the animal jumps forward. Let the children have races. First animal to the top of the string is the winner.

209

GROW FISH

Fold the fish down the middle and cut down the lines. Pull slightly on the fish and watch it grow.

PET ANIMALS & THEIR HOMES

Cut out the pets and their homes. Cut along the dotted lines of the homes. Paste the homes on a piece of paper and place or paste the proper pet inside.

CAT OR DOG MASK

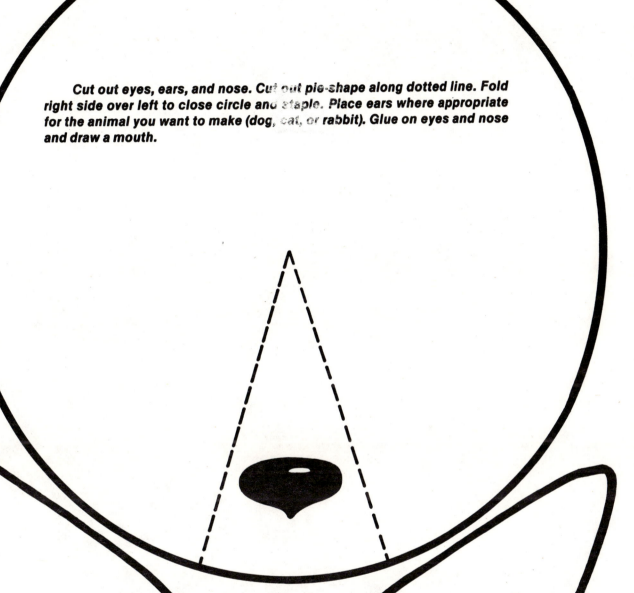

Cut out eyes, ears, and nose. Cut out pie-shape along dotted line. Fold right side over left to close circle and staple. Place ears where appropriate for the animal you want to make (dog, cat, or rabbit). Glue on eyes and nose and draw a mouth.

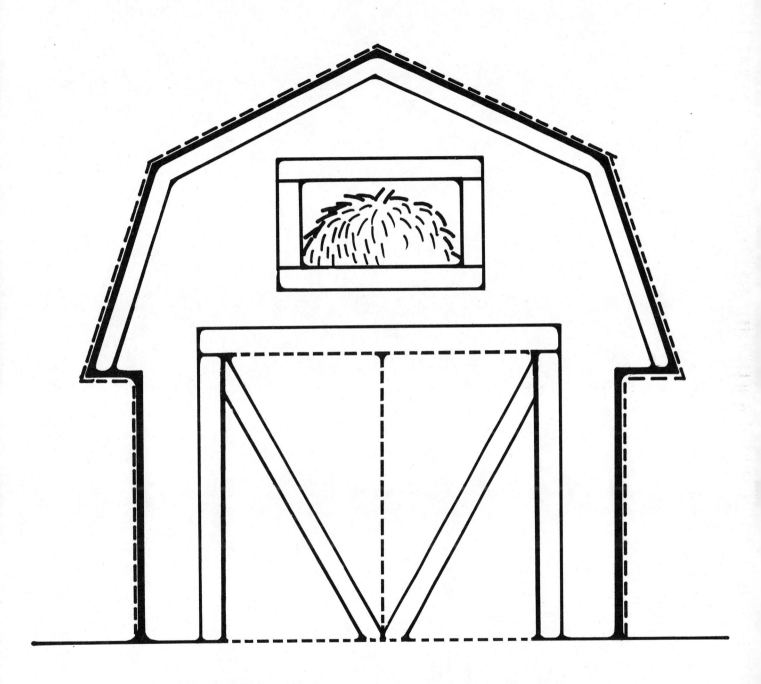

Paste on light cardboard; then cut along dotted lines and fold up, open doors.

BARNYARD ANIMALS

Paste animals on light cardboard before cutting out. Put animal parts together as shown in diagram.

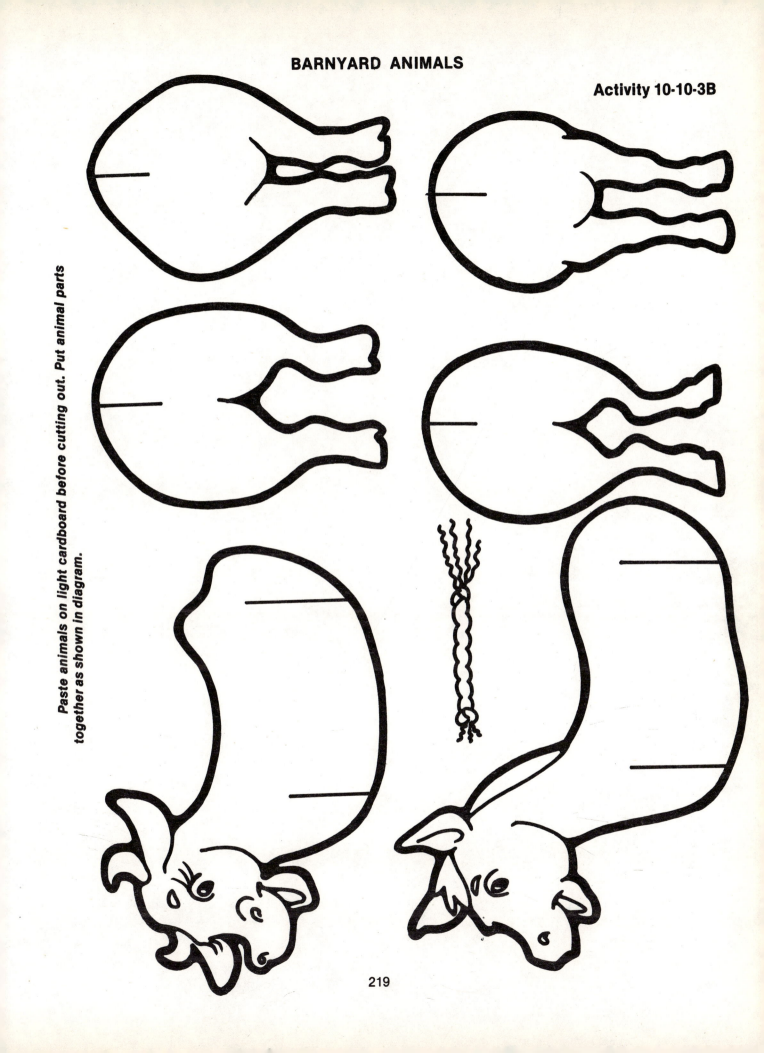

219

WILD ANIMAL BRACELETS

Activity 10-11-2

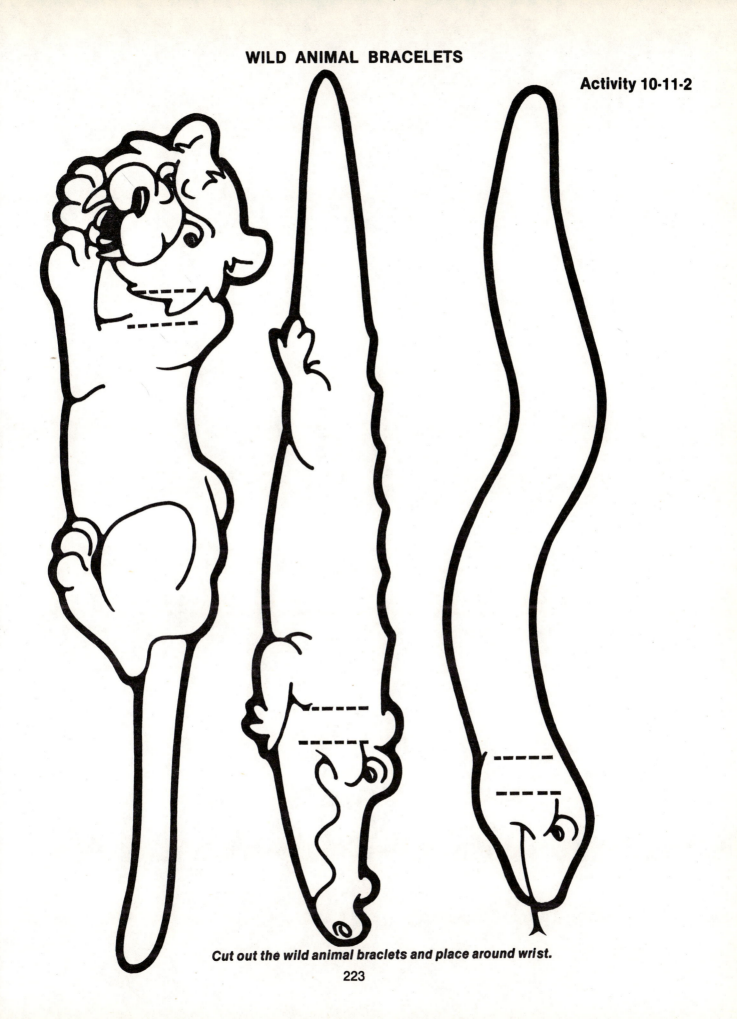

Cut out the wild animal braclets and place around wrist.

BEAR PUPPET

finished
product

Fold sheet of paper in 3rds, cut the top round and glue closed. Paste on features.

GORILLA MARIONETTE

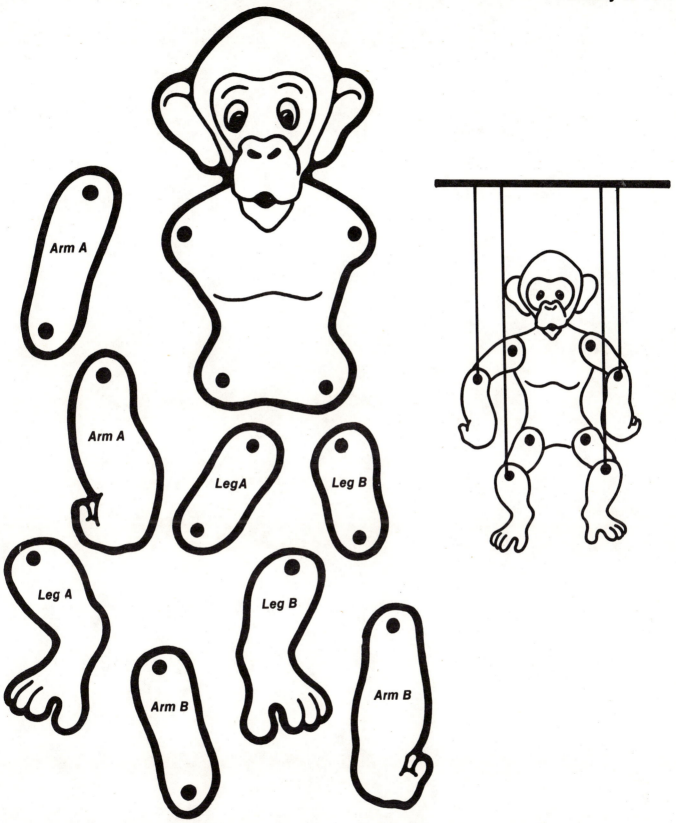

Attach parts of gorilla with brads and string as shown.

227

SQUIRREL PREPARING FOR WINTER

Activity 11-1-7

Pouch—paste on back of cheeks around edges

Cut slit at cheeks on dotted lines. Paste pouch on back of cheeks along edges. Cut out nuts, etc. and stuff in cheeks.

231

PAPER DOLLS

233

WINTER CLOTHES
Dress the paper dolls in their winter attire.

GROUND HOG

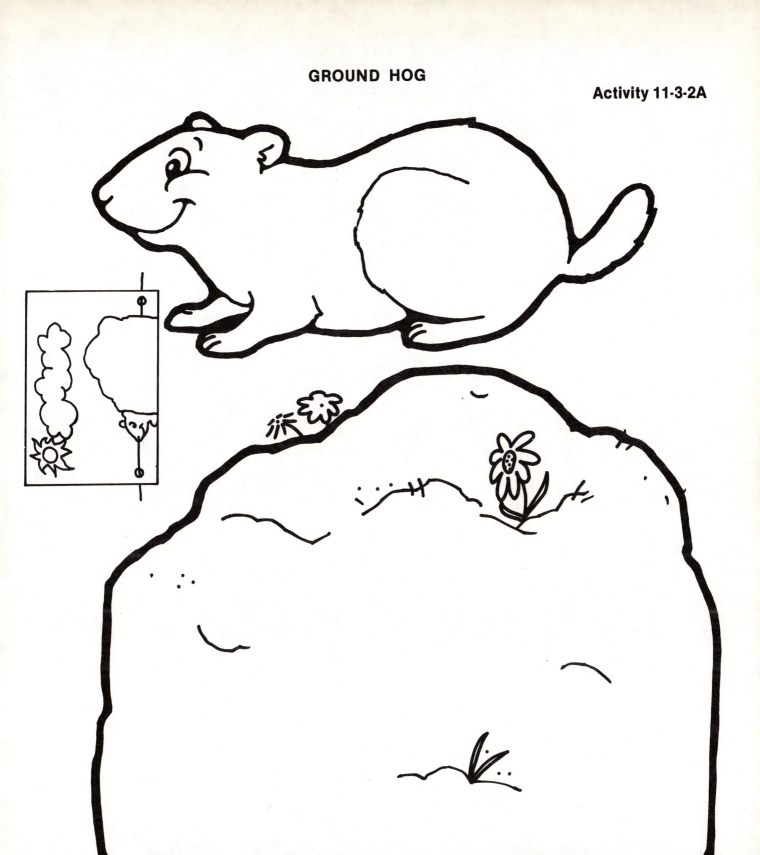

Cut out ground hog and hill house. Paste the top only of the hill securely onto next page below clouds and sun. Cut a string 18 inches long. Tape the center of the string across the back of the ground hog. Punch holes on the side of the page. Thread the ends of the string through the holes and pull the ground hog back and forth, in and out of his hill house.

SPRING CLOTHES

241

WIND TOYS

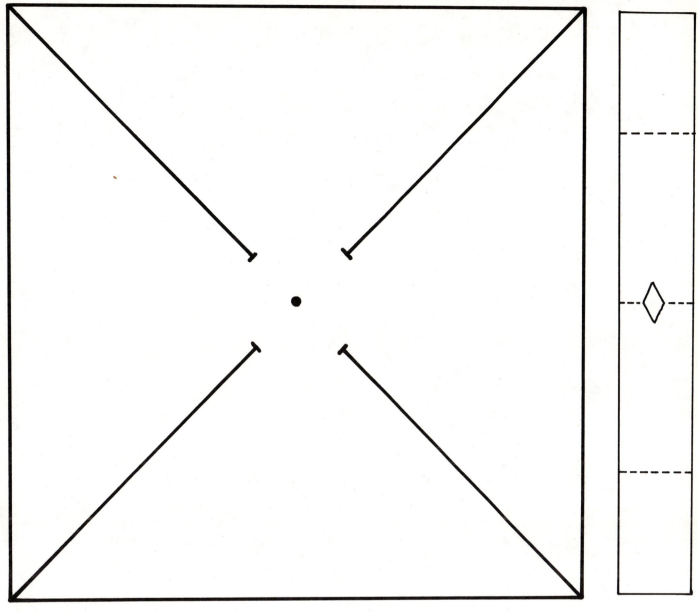

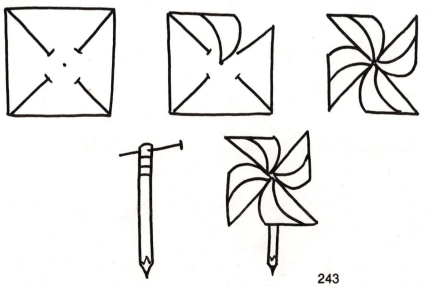

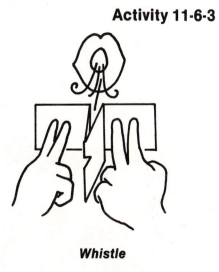

Whistle

SHEEP & COILED SNAKE
Glue cottonballs or popcorn on lamb for his wool.

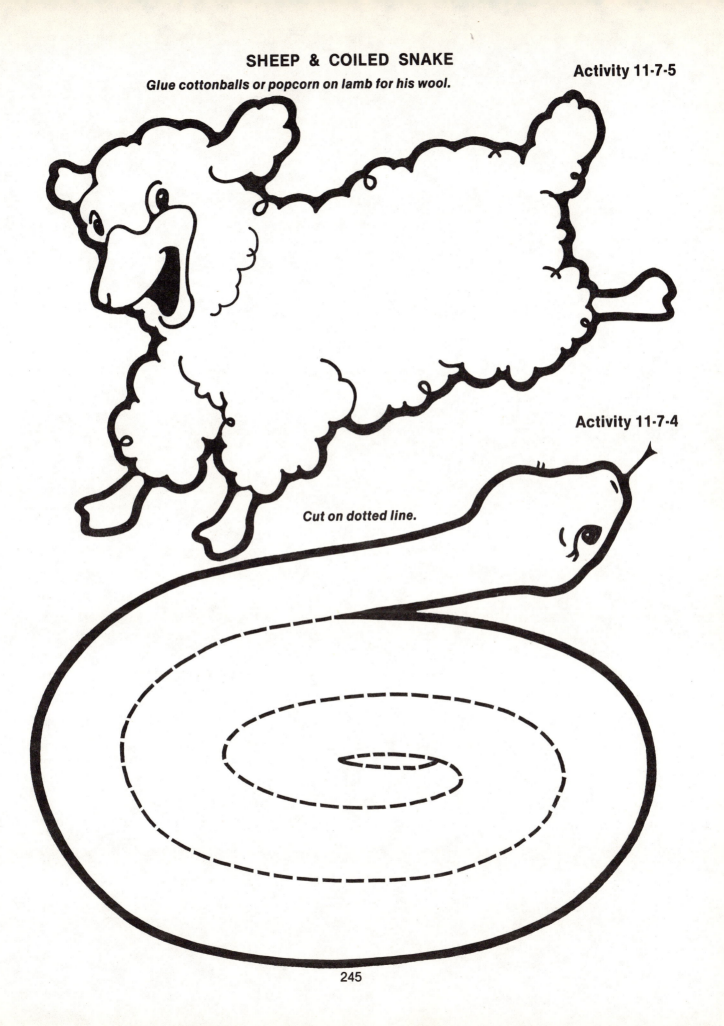

Activity 11-7-4

Cut on dotted line.

HALLOWEEN PICTURE

Circle those things we associate with Halloween. Look closely for the hidden objects.

Cut out and mount on popsicle stick.
Hold up to face as mask.

INDIAN & PAPOOSE

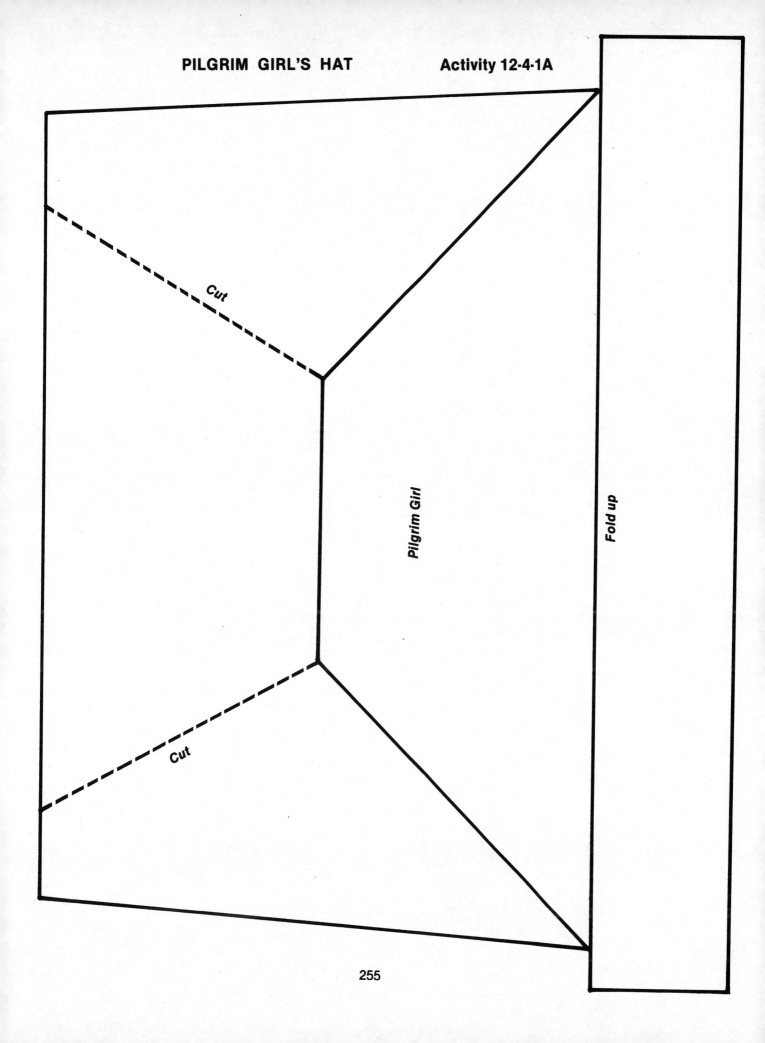

PILGRIM GIRL'S HAT

Activity 12-4-1A

Cut

Cut

Pilgrim Girl

Fold up

255

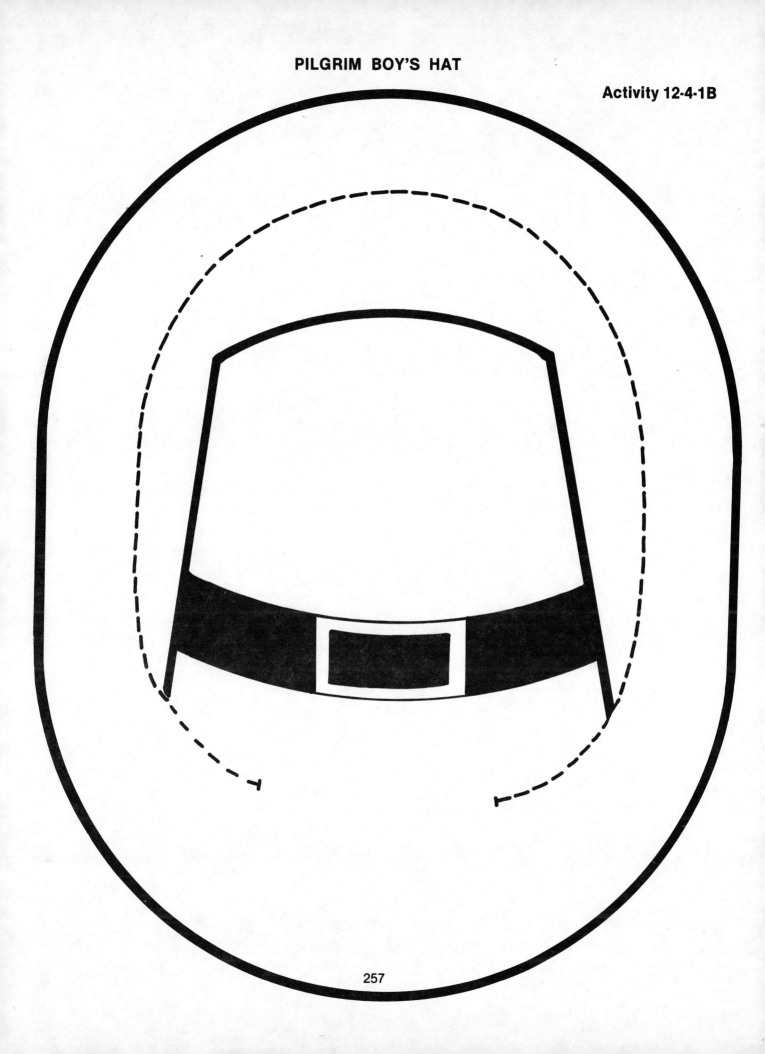

PILGRIM GIRL & BOY

259

PILGRIM CLOTHES

CHRISTMAS SLEIGH

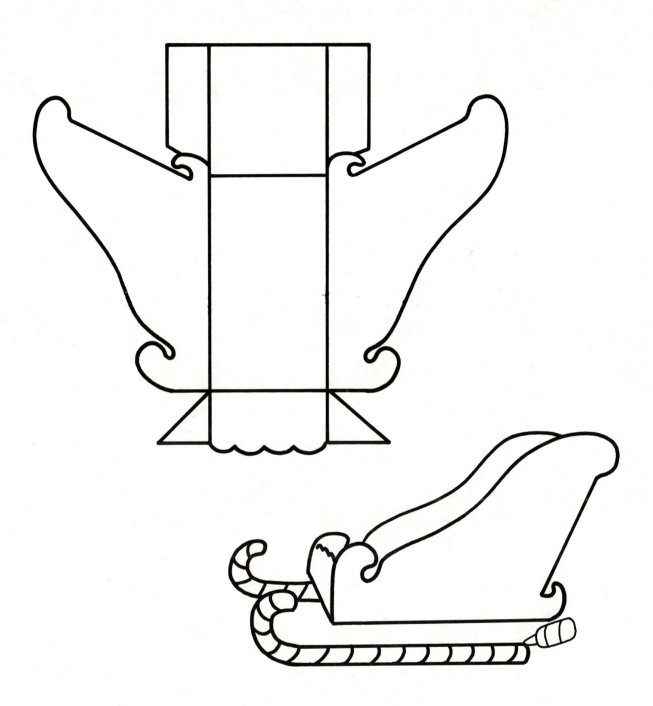

Cut out pattern for sleigh. Fold up the sides and glue tabs on the inside of sleigh. Glue 2 small candy canes as the runners.

Activity 12-6-2

Color, cut out, and place in shoe box for a manger scene.

Color Santa and fill in his beard by glueing on cotton balls or crushed egg shells.

CHRISTMAS STOCKING

Activity 12-6-11

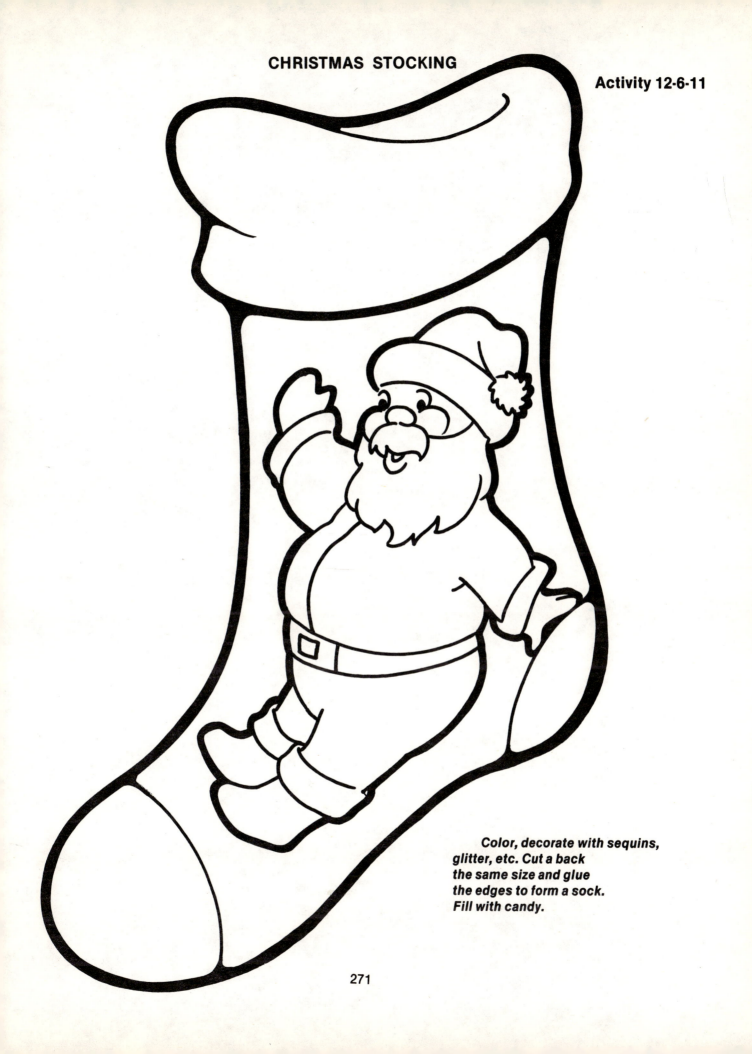

Color, decorate with sequins, glitter, etc. Cut a back the same size and glue the edges to form a sock. Fill with candy.

EASTER PICTURE

Find and color hidden Easter eggs in picture.

DIRECTIONAL WORKSHEET

Circle the animal from the groups on the right that is going the same direction as the animal on the left.

Cut out and glue on staff anywhere child desires.

Circle the musical instrument in each row.

Color, cut out, use as visual aids in singing "Old McDonald had a Farm."

283

Color, cut out, use as visual aids in singing "Old McDonald had a Farm."

Color, cut out, use as visual aids in singing "Old McDonald had a Farm."